MW00784360

Dilemmas in
Educational Leadership

Dilemmas in Educational Leadership

THE FACILITATOR'S BOOK OF CASES

Donna J. Reid

Teachers College
Columbia University
New York and London

Published by Teachers College Press, 1234 Amsterdam Avenue, New York, NY 10027

Copyright © 2014 by Teachers College, Columbia University

All rights reserved. No part of this publication may be reproduced or transmitted in any form or by any means, electronic or mechanical, including photocopy, or any information storage and retrieval system, without permission from the publisher.

Library of Congress Cataloging-in-Publication Data

Reid, Donna J.
  Dilemmas in educational leadership : the facilitator's book of cases / Donna J. Reid.
    p. cm.
  Includes bibliographical references and index.
  ISBN 978-0-8077-5549-5 (pbk. : alk. paper)
  ISBN 978-0-8077-7318-5 (ebook)
  1. Educational leadership—Case studies. 2. Teacher participation in administration.
I. Title.
  LB2805.R45 2014
  371.2—dc23   2014007476

ISBN 978-0-8077-5549-5 (paperback)
ISBN 978-0-8077-7318-5 (eBook)

Printed on acid-free paper
Manufactured in the United States of America

21 20 19 18 17 16 15 14   8 7 6 5 4 3 2 1

To Rob, Elena, and Amanda

Contents

Dilemmas in Educational Leadership

CHAPTER 1

Introduction

With downcast eyes, 12 adults sit in tension-filled silence around a conference table in a spacious school library. Donuts, bags of chocolate, and a tub of soft drinks are set out on a credenza. A handwritten poster with statements such as, "We will collaborate with one another throughout the process," "We will take ownership of our work," and "We will strive to nurture trusting relationships" is hanging from a nearby bookcase. The agenda posted on an easel indicates that the group should be engaged in a text-based discussion about the article "The Zen of Facilitation" (Killion & Simmons, 1992), but one member—their supervisor—has sat huddled in a shawl in total silence for over 45 minutes, and her disengagement has strained the whole group.

Gentle reminders that not everyone has contributed to the conversation have been totally ineffective in encouraging the quieter people to speak up. Instead, even those who were excitedly sharing at first have succumbed to the silence. With its inviting book displays and colorful decorations, this library must be a cheerful place when school is in session, but now the metallic smell of an approaching summer thunderstorm tinges the air, and the gray clouds that can be seen roiling ever closer mirror my own burgeoning frustration.

As the facilitator for this group of principals who are in the middle of a weeklong seminar to help them deepen their collaboration and reflection skills, I wonder: What should I do to address this distressing situation?

If you've ever felt uneasy or unsure about how to fulfill your role as a leader or group facilitator, then this book is for you. The purpose of *Dilemmas in Educational Leadership: The Facilitator's Book of Cases* is to help facilitators and leaders anticipate challenges and prepare for the increased collaboration that is necessary for transforming schools.

THE PROMISE OF COLLABORATIVE COMMUNITIES

Scholars in many fields recognize the value of collaboration. In the corporate world, participation in a "community of practice" can help members coordinate efforts, devise better solutions, and make better decisions (Wenger, McDermott, & Snyder, 2002). Likewise, in education, "knowledge communities" sustain teachers by "providing instruction and opportunities for growth" that can "inspire and influence change" (Craig, 2007, p. 621). Collaboration is not merely a means of lightening the load by sharing work. Rather, it's "an ongoing commitment to make the teaching at the school *better*" (Ellinger, 2008, p. 82).

Professional Learning Communities

The term *professional learning community* (PLC) is often used to describe collaborative groups of educators. Lieberman and Miller (2008) define PLCs as "ongoing groups of teachers who meet regularly for the purpose of increasing their own learning and that of their students" (p. 2), while Hord (2004) explains that "the PLC is not an improvement program or plan, but it provides a structure for schools to continuously improve by building staff capacity for learning and change" (p. 14).

Authors DuFour and Eaker (1998) have popularized the concept of PLCs in North America through seminars and books such as *Professional Learning Communities at Work: Best Practices for Enhancing Student Achievement.* DuFour (2005) bemoans the fact that the label PLC is often used simply to rename grade-level teaching teams, school committees, high school departments, or even an entire school district without actually indicating renewed collaboration or a focus on student learning. For DuFour, the core principles of a professional learning community are ensuring that students learn, creating a culture of collaboration, and focusing on results.

Traits of PLCs

In their studies of what they first called "communities of continuous inquiry and improvement," Hord (2004) and her colleagues at the Southwest Education Development Laboratory identified five dimensions of PLCs: (1) supportive and shared leadership, (2) shared values and vision, (3) collective learning and application of that learning, (4) supportive conditions, and (5) shared personal practice. Lieberman and Miller (2008) determined five interlocking themes in their studies of varied learning communities: (1) context matters; (2) commitments take time to develop; (3) the capacity of members to engage fully in teaching communities grows as commitments develop; (4) content matters, but it has to be balanced with process; and (5) challenges are endemic to any ambitious social enterprise.

Although these particular authors and scholars illuminate PLCs from varied angles, the repeated use of words such as *shared*, *community*, *collective*, and *commitments* across their frameworks indicates that sustained collaboration is foundational to operating as a professional learning community.

Improving Student Outcomes

Evidence continues to mount that educators' engaging in collaborative communities improves student outcomes. For example, through inquiries involving both survey and case studies, researchers in Great Britain have described a positive association between professional learning communities, professional learning, and student achievement (Bolam, McMahon, Stoll, Thomas, & Wallace, 2005). Indeed, students have higher achievement when they attend schools characterized by higher levels of teacher collaboration for school improvement (Goddard, Goddard, & Tschannen-Moran, 2007). Based on their study of teaching contexts in high schools, McLaughlin and Talbert (2001) see "teacher community as a primary unit for improving education quality" (p. 12), and the most effective professional development is characterized by collaboration as well as reflection and multiple opportunities for teacher leadership (Díaz-Maggioli, 2004).

THE CHALLENGES OF COLLABORATION

Even though collaboration is widely recognized as an important attribute of effective schools, the truth is, collaboration is difficult to sustain. Isolation is deeply imbedded in school culture, and the daily realities of schools work against collaboration. In his study of reform movements in Chicago-area schools, Payne (2008) notes that "first-year teachers in urban schools may come expecting trouble with the material or with the children, but they are frequently caught off guard by the difficulty of working with their more experienced colleagues" (p. 20). Even groups that appear to get along well may fall into the trap of remaining "pseudo-communities" (Grossman, Wineburg, & Woolworth, 2001) that suppress conflict and never venture into authentic work.

CRITICAL FRIENDSHIP

My own best learning experiences have been steeped in supportive relationships. During my difficult first years as a 7th-grade history teacher, I was surrounded by supportive professionals who patiently listened, advised, and modeled a better way. My veteran teammates met daily to swap stories about our students, plan interdisciplinary lessons, and communicate with parents. My department chair wholeheartedly welcomed me, and another Texas history teacher gave me unlimited access to his file cabinets stuffed with creative lesson plans. I struggled with how to engage all of my diverse students and could easily have turned into one of the 50% of new teachers who leave the profession within 5 years (Ingersoll & Smith, 2003). Instead, these professional relationships nurtured my professional learning, and I grew into new roles as a team leader, department chair, and critical friends group (CFG) coach.

Critical Friends Groups

Rooted in the research of scholars who have explored the importance of teacher collaboration and reflection in improving classroom practice—such as Milbrey McLaughlin, Joan Talbert, Judith Warren Little, Fred Newmann, and Karen Seashore Louis—critical friends groups (CFGs) are a special type of professional learning community that emerged in the early 1990s. Characterized by the use of discussion-based protocols and an emphasis on skilled facilitation and coaching, CFGs operate at the intersection of adult learning, organizational culture, school change, and transformational learning (Fahey & Ippolito, 2014). Critical friends groups are supported at the national level by the School Reform Initiative (SRI), an organization that promotes the creation of transformational learning communities fiercely committed to educational equity and excellence.

Transformational Learning

My involvement in critical friendship truly transformed my teaching practice by teaching me how to be more reflective and introducing me to powerful tools for collaboration such as setting group norms, composing thoughtful agendas, and using protocols to make conversations more reflective and equitable. More important, my experiences in CFGs made me more aware of tensions that riddle educational policy and practice. In a landmark keynote address, CFG cocreator Gene Thompson-Grove (2005) described ways in which CFGs are in opposition to traditional, positivistic formats for professional development and policymaking:

> We [CFG coaches] are going against the tide of governmental and other policy organizations that pretend there is one right answer and one quick fix—that issues in education can be reduced to one solution, can be fixed by one-size-fits-all

legislation. We know better. Faced with standardization—we willingly embrace, grapple with, and hold the messiness, ambiguity, and questions that arise when the human dynamic is involved.

Thompson-Grove lifts up CFGs as "one of the few reform efforts that truly empowers teachers to be authors of their own learning, that gives them the capacity to assume leadership around issues that really matter in schools and districts."

In the spirit of critical friendship, *Dilemmas in Educational Leadership: The Facilitator's Book of Cases* is designed to develop and strengthen collaboration skills so you can have the conversations that "really matter," whether those conversations take place in a CFG, a PLC, a team meeting, or simply over coffee in the teachers' lounge.

THE NEED FOR THIS BOOK

Although the advantages of collaboration are clear, when educators are rubbing shoulders instead of working in isolation, friction is inevitable. Yet very little of the current literature warns educators about what kinds of tensions to expect or how to navigate through the unavoidable "messiness, ambiguity, and questions" that Thompson-Grove mentions. Many resources are available that explain the importance of incorporating focused, educator-led reflective groups into a school (Conzemius & O'Neill, 2001; DuFour & Eaker, 1998). Others describe the kinds of conversations that these groups can engage in to improve teacher practice and student learning (McDonald, Mohr, Dichter, & McDonald, 2007; Venables, 2011) or touch on the challenges of facilitating protocols (Allen & Blythe, 2004). But when groups encounter discord based on irritating interpersonal situations, clashing work styles, or conflicting values, the best intentions for collaboration can collapse under the weight of the group's inexperience, discomfort, or downright fear. DuFour, DuFour, and Eaker (2008) forcefully write, "It is impossible for a school or district to develop the capacity to function as a professional learning community without undergoing profound cultural shifts" (p. 91), and a group's cultural shifts depend on the leadership and collaborative capacity of many individuals.

Since I was first trained to lead other teachers as a critical friends group coach in 1998, I have coached several CFGs, trained and supported dozens of CFG coaches, and facilitated at countless regional and national professional development venues. After my initial training, I soon became adept at convening groups, developing meeting agendas, and selecting protocols to build trust and encourage meaningful conversations. I found myself adapting and using these skills in a wide variety of contexts as a classroom teacher, department chair, consultant, and community leader outside of schools. However, even after developing my basic facilitation skills, situations continued to crop up— like in the opening vignette of this introduction—which left me flummoxed:

- How could I balance my nonconfrontational demeanor and identity as a "nice" person with the responsibility of keeping the group on track?
- How could I nurture trusting relationships in groups that had powerful members who withdrew or shut down?
- And how in the world could I open a space for my colleagues to have important conversations about equity, poverty, and power when there is currently so much pressure to focus all school conversations on benchmarks and test scores?

WHAT THIS BOOK INCLUDES

Anthropologist Mary Catherine Bateson (1994) writes, "Our species thinks in metaphors and learns through stories" (p. 11), and *Dilemmas in Educational Leadership: The Facilitator's Book of Cases* features 10 stories related to the leadership and facilitation of school-based collaborative groups. Cases that shed light on the inner workings of teacher learning communities already appear in qualitative research literature (Achinstein, 2002; Curry, 2008; Grossman, Wineburg, & Woolworth, 2001; Wood, 2007), but the narratives in *Dilemmas in Educational Leadership* are more accessible and are optimized to help you make connections with your own practice. This book offers an avenue for teachers, principals, content specialists, professional developers, and others to practice and reflect on the kinds of skills they will need to guide a successful learning community.

Designed to be read in any order, the main chapters of *Dilemmas in Educational Leadership: The Facilitator's Book of Cases* present fictionalized narrative cases with conflicts and feelings drawn from real-life experiences. By retaining the complexity of real school contexts, these cases show how educators develop their practical knowledge about collaboration, facilitation, and leadership (Clandinin & Connelly, 1995). Chapters 2 through 11 each begin with the key topics and challenges in the chapter, and each case is followed by a set of questions to help you frame the problems therein, identify the specific facilitation moves that arose in the narrative, and reflect about what alternatives are possible.

The cases in Part I, "Learning New Habits," cover basic facilitation skills and challenges that have to be faced when educators are first embarking on collaborative work, such as how to develop new skills in facilitating, questioning, and listening. Part II, "Building Relationships for Sustainability," tackles interpersonal skills such as engaging reluctant team members, dealing with difficult people, and working through conflict. Part III, "Exploring Tensions," delves into some of the most pernicious dilemmas that can stymie even experienced teacher leaders and facilitators. These difficult problems touch on themes such as negotiating time to meet, respecting confidentiality, and developing cultural competence. Part IV, "Tying It All Together," weaves together the several threads that emerge in the cases and provides a discussion of the theory that underlies these powerful practices. Finally, the book includes supporting materials such as a compilation of further resources and tables that highlight facilitative leadership practices and their possible implications for each case.

HOW TO USE THIS BOOK

A case is simply a narrative, and good cases are complex enough to have multiple levels of analysis and multiple interpretations. My work is grounded in a tradition that believes that teacher knowledge is formed in community and is dependent on context (Clandinin et al., 2006; Craig, 2003; Dewey, 1938). Furthermore, teachers acquire the bulk of their professional knowledge through continuous action and reflection on everyday problems (Schön, 1987). Case studies are a means for educators to develop their personal practical knowledge by reading and discussing the cases together.

First, read a case and make note of key facts and any questions that you have. The chapters are arranged in a way that puts similar dilemmas together, but you may read the cases in any order.

Second, analyze the case. Ask yourself: What is the context of this particular group? What relationships are involved? What are the critical moments when the facilitator had to make decisions? Generate a list of alternative actions that group members might have taken and think about which alternatives might be more effective. There are prompts and questions at the end of each chapter to help you get started with your analysis, and these are arranged around the reflective prompts, "*What? So what? Now what?*"

The "*What*" questions ask us to sharpen our observation skills by simply noticing and describing what happened in the case without making any judgments. The "*So what*" questions ask us to reflect on the implications of the actions of the featured facilitators, while the "*Now what*" prompts encourage us to make connections with our own experiences, think of alternatives, and internalize the stories so we can transform our own facilitative practice.

Also, for each chapter, readers can refer to Appendix A both for sample answers to the question of what happened in the cases and more questions to spark further group discussion. The tables in Appendix A should not be interpreted as the definitive way to make meaning of the case. Instead, they are simply meant to be starting places for discussion and extra support for those readers who are new to facilitation.

Third, share your responses and questions with others and listen carefully to their contributions so your tool chest of facilitative leadership skills will become even more diverse and effective. Although you can read and reflect on these cases by yourself, I strongly encourage you to use them as the basis of small-group discussions because "just as a piece of music exists only partially when it isn't being sung or played, a case comes fully to life only when it's being discussed" (Hansen, 1987, p. 265, as cited in Merseth, 1996, p. 727).

I firmly believe that the expertise for solving dilemmas usually lies with those closest to the problem. My hope is that by reading and discussing the cases, you will build your own capacity to effectively guide groups through the challenges that undermine our best intentions for sustained collaboration and reflection.

ACKNOWLEDGMENTS

I would like to acknowledge the following critical friends who have offered much-needed and much-appreciated inspiration, encouragement, and feedback over the course of this project: Carley Colton, Cheryl Craig, Gayle Curtis, Sossiena Demissie-Sanders, Terri Goodman, Janet Gray, Michaelann Kelley, Tim Martindell, Mary Matthews, Jonett Miniel, Lee Mountain, Mike Pérez, Liz Peterson, Lydia Smith, and Maggie Trendell.

Learning New Habits

The three cases in Part I are told from the point of view of Andrea, a newly trained critical friends group coach who is facilitating a group of teaching peers at her middle school campus for the very first time. Andrea and her colleagues encounter several challenges as they work together throughout the year. Chapter 2, "Becoming a Facilitator," describes Andrea's first few months of facilitation and the frustration that comes with developing new skills. Chapter 3, "Becoming Questioners," deals with taking on the hard work of examining student work and asking difficult questions about one's own teaching practice. Chapter 4, "Becoming Listeners," highlights using protocols to enhance professional conversations and takes on the challenge of overcoming resistance to protocol-based reflective learning.

Becoming a Facilitator

Key Topics: novice facilitator, reflective practice, professional identity, Consultancy protocol, philosophy of facilitation

Key Challenges: feeling inadequate in a new role, identifying and strengthening facilitation skills

CONTEXT

As part of a schoolwide initiative to encourage more reflective practice and enhance the school's professional learning communities, the administration of Monroe Middle School has instituted voluntary critical friends groups that meet for 2 hours once a month after school. About half of the faculty chose to participate, and Andrea is one of the four faculty coaches who were trained over the summer to lead a group. Almost halfway into the year, Andrea is disappointed by the lackluster efforts of her group but doesn't know what to do about it. What skills and dispositions does Andrea need to be a more effective facilitator, and how can she develop those skills?

ANDREA SPEAKS ABOUT HER EXPERIENCE

I've been teaching 6th-grade world cultures at Monroe Middle School for 5 years now. When I heard that our principal was seeking critical friends training for the staff, I was thrilled. The way I understand it, a critical friends group, or CFG, is special because it is teacher-led professional development that is based on our own questions about our own practice. Our 80-person faculty is already fairly collaborative. The core subject teachers have an extra planning period each day for meeting with our interdisciplinary teams, and I've learned a great deal from my teammates who teach math, science, and English to the same students I have for social studies. I've also heard that, compared with

Critical Friends Group

some of the surrounding schools, we here at Monroe also have strong departments that try to continually improve instruction in the content areas. Still, our principal wanted us to attend CFG training so we could learn some new tools to take our collaborative and reflective work deeper.

Four faculty members from Monroe took the 5-day training back in June and it exceeded my expectations. I was in awe of our four training facilitators from around the country, who seemed so experienced and wise as they seamlessly led us from activity to activity—all the while gently prodding us to think more deeply. Split into four smaller home groups, the 60 participants got to know our colleagues from around the region really well. Together we set norms, engaged in team-building activities, discussed articles about school reform, learned how to use protocols to learn from student work, and reflected regularly about what we were learning and how it might change our practice as teachers and teacher leaders. Every day was rich with new learning. We were not just learning new techniques for leading a group; we were learning about ourselves and our colleagues.

What was especially empowering was the idea that a critical friends group was a teacher-led inquiry group. We brought our own work to the table and asked the questions that were important to us—not just what the principal or the school board or the testing corporations thought was important. By the end of the week, I had embraced the identities of teacher as thinker, inquirer, facilitator, and leader rather than the dominant metaphor of teacher as a mere technician.

When the four trained CFG coaches from Monroe returned to school in August, we got 15 minutes at a faculty meeting to share our experiences from the summer training. Because our presentation was so enthusiastic, it was easy to recruit 40 faculty members to be in our new CFGs.

FEELING DISAPPOINTED

After such a powerful experience this summer, I can't help but feel a little disappointed about how my own group is progressing. The principal claims that she randomly placed the interested faculty members into groups, and I believe it because the 10 of us don't have anything in common besides working in the same building. Barbara, the current technology teacher who used to teach home economics, has been at Monroe for decades. Lori and Heather are 1st-year teachers. Four of us teach some level of social studies, and the others teach technology, math, English, English as a Second Language, and Spanish. Wanda, the part-time speech therapist, rounds out the group.

We meet once a month after school lets out, and I'm leaning heavily on the agendas from the summer training sessions to plan our current meetings. In September, we set group norms after we wrote about the conditions we needed to do our best learning, discussed a short article about giving and receiving feedback, and passed around a sign-up sheet for bringing snacks and drinks to all the meetings this year. In October, we did a fun team builder, and I presented some of my own work for feedback. For our November meeting, my group met in Heather's classroom and noshed on cheese, crackers, veggies, and hummus while we unwound for a bit and then dove into the agenda. We discussed another article and Tracy shared one of her English tests for us to examine.

We write reflections at the close of each meeting, and I use these to gauge what the group is learning and make adjustments for next month's meeting. Just like in the summer training, I use the prompts, "What worked? What didn't work? What do you need?" Here's a taste of what I saw when I read the reflections from our third meeting in November:

Carlos: We accomplished much communication and
positive interaction. The group might need more
openness and perhaps a sense of humor.
Tracy: Good attention to time. Good discussion (though a bit stiff).
Barbara: I liked how the protocol for the article
discussion was very effective.
Wanda: I enjoyed the informality of the group. Although we
became structured, I felt that I had the freedom to agree and
disagree with peers in a calm environment. What didn't work—
very tired after work—sometimes couldn't think clearly.
Lori: What worked? Starting and ending on time. Sharing of
experience positively. What I need? More sharing of ideas
that can help me professionally as well as personally.
Heather: I liked the structure, openness, Andrea's
organization, and the timing.

They didn't write anything about how they might change their classroom practice or how they were opening up to new ways of thinking about schooling. Even though I was leading the same kinds of activities that I had experienced in the summer, my group members were not having a transformative experience. It seemed like what they most admired was my time management, but I had a sinking feeling that we were not going to have transformative experiences just by showing up on time.

USING A CONSULTANCY TO GET HELP

Fortunately, the 60 participants from our CFG training seminar were scheduled to soon have a mini-reunion and support session. Getting to present our own dilemmas of practice was part of the agenda.

We met on Saturday morning at a nearby university that donated space in its student center for our 1-day get-together. I gravitated to the other members of my home group, whom I'd come to trust during our intense training in June.

When it was time to discuss our dilemmas using the Consultancy protocol (Dunne, Evans, & Thompson-Grove, cited in School Reform Initiative, 2014), I volunteered to share my dilemma. Simon, a math teacher from a neighboring high school, volunteered to facilitate the protocol. I gave an overview of my dilemma and passed out meeting agendas and written reflections, with the names removed, for the group to examine. My framing question was, "How can I push my group to a have a more transformative critical friends experience?"

The group quietly examined the agendas and reflections that I had brought, and Simon kept the group on track while they asked a few clarifying and probing questions. Then I sat back and listened while the small group talked about my dilemma.

Betty spoke first: "I understand why she's disappointed, but it's still very early in the year. Andrea's group has had three meetings. That's just 6 or 7 hours together. That's like the end of our first day of training. No one was transforming after just 6 hours. It's going to take more time."

"Yeah," Gabe added. "Andrea shouldn't be so hard on herself. We had such an amazing experience last summer, but we were immersed in the training. The seminar was at a hotel instead of a school campus. We ate gourmet meals. We didn't have to go home and grade papers. One of her group members even wrote that she can't think clearly after a long day at work. I think it's easier to engage in professional learning when you're not distracted by the day-to-day stuff."

Marcy chimed in, "Some of the coaches here today haven't even had their first meeting. I'm impressed that Andrea's group has met three times and has made examining student work a priority."

"It's good to acknowledge that Andrea's coaching work has some strengths," Simon intervened. "But she wants our help with getting her group to go deeper. What suggestions can we offer?"

"I wonder if Andrea really knows what they are learning," said Gabe. "The reflection prompts seem limiting. When she asks, 'What worked?

What didn't work? and What do you need?' she's just getting comments about her facilitation."

Marcy added, "Kudos to Andrea for remembering to have her group write reflections at the end of each meeting, but I think she could move on to some different reflective prompts. The blue book that came with our training materials, *The Facilitator's Book of Questions* (Allen & Blythe, 2004), suggests learning, logistics, and longevity. If Andrea wants to encourage transformation, she should ask about what they are learning at the meetings and what changes they might make because of the meetings. Transformation is so personal. How can she get inside their heads?"

Betty jumped back in, "Yeah, changing the prompts for the written reflections is an important step, but it's not enough. From the reflection excerpts that Andrea brought, I wonder if the group even understands why they are meeting."

I wanted to interrupt and explain all the ways that the four new coaches at Monroe had communicated the purposes of the CFGs, but Simon put his hand on my forearm and reminded me that I should just listen and take notes. My time to respond would come later.

Marcy added, "I agree with Betty that it might help the group go deeper if they had an explicit conversation about why they are there. Maybe a 3-column KWL chart where they list what they *know* about CFGs in the first column and what they *want* to know in the next. The 'L' column, what they are *learning*, could be filled in at the end of each meeting. Put it on chart paper, roll it up, and bring it back each month."

"Or do an affinity map around the question 'What do I hope to get out of this learning community?'" suggested Gabe. "Maybe some people just want to be there to socialize and others want to pick up a few tricks and tips for the classroom. I doubt that transforming their core beliefs about teaching and learning has crossed their minds."

Betty noted, "From the agendas that Andrea shared with us, it looks like she has chosen readings from our summer training that were about school-reform stuff. What might happen if she included some short articles about reflective practice or equity or something that pushed the group members' thinking a little more?"

Simon reminded the group that they had just a couple of minutes left and pointed to my focusing question that he had posted on the wall. Marcy had the last word: "Facilitation is a new experience for all of us. It's different from teaching. We are in uncharted territory, and the objectives aren't clear-cut. I wonder if Andrea has written out her philosophy of facilitation. What are the values that guide her work? If she could nail that down—if we could all nail that down—then we'd have guideposts for our journeys as facilitators."

Simon looked down at his timer and brought that step of the consultancy to a close. It was then my turn to respond.

NEW UNDERSTANDINGS

With gratitude, I told my colleagues how their comments had provided a fresh perspective. Through their eyes, I saw that my novice CFG needed more time together and that my group was always physically tired when we met, so that affected their engagement. The consultancy helped me realize that my understanding of facilitation had been too narrow. I needed to be much more than a convener and timekeeper. I was eager to experiment with the prompts for the written reflections so I could get more useful feedback that went beyond meeting logistics. Finally, when I looked at the reflections again, I saw that my CFG had articulated a strong foundation of "positive interaction," "freedom to agree and disagree," and "sharing of experience." I was inspired to revisit the purpose of our CFG and trust that the group would find its own direction. I also promised to take Marcy's advice and write down my philosophy of facilitation. We laughed together when I wondered out loud why we hadn't done that back in June.

ANDREA'S PHILOSOPHY OF FACILITATION

After our mini-reunion ended, I continued to mull things over. Later that evening, I scratched out a few bullet points of why I believe that critical friendship and facilitation are so important:

- I believe that teaching is intellectual, creative, and relational work.
- I believe that all teachers, no matter how experienced, have something to learn.
- I believe that teachers, as the adults who actually work with students every day, are best positioned to ask the kinds of questions that really matter to improving teaching and learning.
- I believe that good professional development is relational. Teachers learn by talking to one another.
- I believe that a facilitator can optimize how teachers learn from one another.
- I believe that using protocols can help me be a more skilled facilitator.
- I believe that learning how to use protocols is not enough to be a skilled facilitator.

- I believe that there is no one best way to teach or facilitate, but it is a facilitator's job to create a safe and respectful setting where difficult conversations can take place.

By questioning my practice and getting input from others, I understood that it was laughable to ever think that a 5-day seminar would be enough training to facilitate independently. I need more time to practice. At least now I feel more comfortable and confident about becoming a better facilitator. I'll continue to create a nurturing environment where we can bring our own work and our students' work to the table, but I am letting go of my preconceived notions and timetable about what my group members must believe.

Chapter 2 Discussion Questions

What?

1. Describe Andrea's facilitation context: Who is in her group? When do they meet? What do they do during meetings?
2. Describe Andrea's facilitation training.

So What?

3. What causes Andrea to doubt herself?

Now What?

4. What resources do you use to become a better facilitator?
5. Write down your own philosophy of facilitation. Why do you value facilitation or facilitative leadership? What do you bring to the people you facilitate? Why is your work important?

Becoming Questioners

> *Key Topics:* teacher inquiry, professional relationships, reflective
> practice, looking at student work, dilemmas
>
> *Key Challenges:* balancing the multiple purposes of a professional
> learning community, challenging peers in a respectful atmosphere

CONTEXT

A young teacher who has taken on the challenge of facilitating a critical friends group of fellow teachers at her middle school, Andrea, continues to struggle with how to push her colleagues to ask the kinds of questions about their practice that could lead to real changes in their classrooms. One member of the group especially values having a supportive atmosphere and resists activities that might lead to discomfort or expose differences in opinion. How can Andrea encourage her group to take up serious questions about teaching and learning, even if the process is sometimes uncomfortable?

ANDREA SPEAKS ABOUT HER EXPERIENCE

The administrators of Monroe Middle School established four voluntary CFGs this year in order to strengthen our faculty's reflective practice. Before school started in August, the four newly trained group facilitators recruited our coworkers into the new CFGs by giving a short presentation at a faculty meeting. Along with the other coaches, I explained how critical friends groups could revive our collaborative spirit and give us a venue for getting feedback. All the interested teachers and staff signed up, and our principal assigned each participant to a group. When the principal distributed the group rosters, I was thrilled to see that Barbara had been placed in my group because I have admired and appreciated her since my very first week at Monroe Middle School.

Barbara and I met 5 years ago over lunch in the teachers' lounge. With one glance, she could tell whenever I was agitated or overwhelmed. I felt safe sharing my frustrations with her, and her wisdom and gentle encouragement often gave me the boost I needed to make it through the rest of the day. The whole faculty knows that Barbara is a caretaker. Feeling chilled? There's an extra sweater in her closet. Have a headache? Barbara will readily share her acetaminophen and ibuprofen. With decades of teaching experience in fields ranging from self-contained elementary to home economics to computer literacy, she was like another mother to me. I call her my professional aunt.

As expected, Barbara fills the same caretaking roll in our critical friends group. When it was her turn to bring snacks to our after-school meeting, Barbara didn't just bring a package of cookies and 2-liter bottles of soda like most of us. Instead, she prepared fruit salad, a sandwich tray, and freshly brewed iced tea. Her thoughtfulness and generosity make her a beloved asset to our CFG.

LEARNING FROM STUDENT WORK

Besides enjoying friendly professional relationships, what made the critical friends training so transformative for me was looking at student work and examining authentic teaching dilemmas. Whenever it was my turn to present a problem during the training seminar, I felt empowered by the process of reflecting on my students' work, choosing a problem, framing a focusing question, and getting helpful feedback from my peers. I wanted my own CFG members to have that same powerful experience, so I incorporated looking at student work sessions into our monthly agendas as soon as possible.

Presenting My Own Work

For my group's first experience with closely examining student work, I decided to bring in samples of a group geography project that I had assigned for 3 years in a row. The assignment was to create a travel brochure about a particular region in the world. Even though I kept tinkering with the assignment, I was disappointed in the results because my students turned in brochures that were factually accurate but not very polished. The writing lacked verve, and many brochures were not at all visually appealing. How could I provide clear expectations and support the students' success?

It was difficult for me to both present work and facilitate the protocol, but I thought it was important to model putting my own work on the table for discussion. We used the Tuning protocol (McDonald & Allen, cited in School Reform Initiative, 2014) to examine the samples. During a Tuning protocol, the presenting teacher describes the context for the work and her expectations. She provides a focusing question, and the group members ask clarifying questions to make sure they understand the context and standards. Then the group examines the work and offers warm and cool feedback while the presenter listens and takes notes. Through their warm feedback, my peers helped me recognize positive traits about the assignment, such as the way it encouraged creativity, and Geraldine said she liked how I had "leveled the playing field" for the students by providing time in class to complete the project.

My critical friends also freely gave cool feedback that helped me see the gaps in my instruction. For example, I should have shared the scoring rubric with the students ahead of time so they would be aware that I valued pizzazz as well as accuracy. Tracy, the English teacher, pointed out that the students had lost focus of who the audience was, and it would be helpful if I made the audience more explicit for the students, since a travel brochure must be persuasive as well as factual. She also suggested asking for the writing ahead of time and spending some class time with peer editing. When it was my turn to respond, I shared how both the warm and cool feedback in the Tuning protocol inspired me to improve the assignment for my students.

Because Heather—one of the new teachers—wrote, "The Tuning protocol really worked. I wish we could do this all the time. I loved it. I always need help with feedback on work" in her post-meeting reflections, I felt like we were well on the way to all of us asking questions about our instruction.

Skepticism

In November, Tracy brought a test from her English class for us to examine. The exam questions were mostly open ended and students could choose which questions to answer. Tracy valued giving the students choices so they could maximize their strengths, but that made grading the test papers more difficult. We used the Consultancy protocol (Dunne, Evans, & Thompson-Grove, cited in School Reform Initiative, 2014) to explore her dilemma of wanting to evaluate student learning fairly while providing student choice. After Tracy gave an overview of her dilemma, the group members asked clarifying questions to make sure that we understood Tracy's context and then we asked probing questions that helped Tracy see her dilemma from different points of view.

Then Tracy silently took notes while we discussed the issues and offered suggestions. We found that Tracy's dilemma got to the heart of issues such as the purpose of grades and what makes a grade fair.

The reactions to this session were mixed. Tracy reflected that she felt very self-conscious at first, yet she appreciated the "supportive input." Most group members liked the process of the protocol, but some questioned whether it truly helped the presenter. One member wrote, "Although I don't think we helped Tracy a whole lot, I enjoyed the process. It is interesting to learn great ways of giving feedback."

Vulnerability

In order to address my earlier concerns about the CFG not going deep enough (see Chapter 2), the bulk of the December meeting was spent addressing the purpose of the CFG. We then dedicated about 45 minutes to a Tuning protocol for Heather, one of the new teachers at Monroe Middle School. Heather brought an essay assignment from her advanced world cultures class and asked for input about how to improve the handouts. She was disappointed that the essays were not fully developed even though she provided a detailed format on the assignment sheet.

As I had done 2 months before, Heather brought in the teacher-made assignment sheet and several student work samples. As facilitator, I felt challenged when Geraldine blurted out, "Why is she expecting 11-year-olds to write abstract college essays? Her kids probably need more activity!" with a laughing tone, and Heather flinched. I don't think that Geraldine is mean; she just words things poorly sometimes. I reminded everybody of our feedback norms that were posted on the wall, and that seemed to smooth the ruffled feelings.

During the debriefing, we talked about how the discussion had surfaced issues related to teaching writing across the curriculum. Together, we saw that we had varied expectations and that there were many inconsistencies at Monroe Middle School in how teachers incorporated writing skills into their assignments. I wondered if we should pursue a discussion that aired our different experiences and expectations, but our time was up.

At the end of the meeting, Barbara smiled and said, "I would like to present at our meeting in January. I have something that I think would be really helpful to the group."

I was puzzled by her reference to being "helpful," but knew that we could sort it all out when the two of us got together for a preconference after winter break.

PREPARING FOR THE NEXT MEETING

As usual, I read the participants' written reflections from the previous meeting to prepare for the next. A couple of people, including Barbara, voiced concern about the incident in which Geraldine had laughed at Heather's work. On the other hand, I felt encouraged that Geraldine, a rather hard-bitten veteran, wrote, "Keep up your cool spirit, Andrea. The slow pace and good technique are working even with me. I'm learning to listen more."

Tracy's insightful reflection had the most impact on my thinking. She stated, "Heather brought in a question that was too narrow and an assignment that had too few flaws. We should feel comfortable to bring in flawed work in order to improve ourselves. I need to feel as if this group really is going to make a difference in the school." I was so grateful that Tracy was getting it. This comment perfectly encapsulated what I wanted our group to accomplish: providing a place to learn and grow as teachers—a place that was "friendly" but didn't shrink from doing "critical" work. I was determined that our CFG meetings would balance safety with productive risk-taking. I left for winter break feeling energized and confident about the work that we could accomplish.

EMERGING FRUSTRATION

When we returned to school in January, I sent Barbara a short email asking her when she would like to have a preconference so we could chat about the work she would bring, choose an appropriate protocol, and develop a focusing question. Barbara and I met in the computer lab after school, and she told me her idea for presenting work.

"Andrea, I volunteered to show some of my work because the part of these meetings that I like best is the sharing of ideas. I think all the teachers learn a lot from each other when we see what one another's students are doing."

"That's great, Barbara. So tell me about the work you would like to bring to the group."

"Well, I thought that this would be a great time to show everybody how to use the technology we have at Monroe to develop digital writing assignments. Have you noticed that the dilemmas that you and Tracy and Heather brought all had a writing component? I'd love to show the group how to improve student engagement by using the tablets or using online document editing. You can also personalize learning with our technological resources. The possibilities are endless."

"What do you want feedback on? What's your question?"

"I don't need feedback. I just want to share."

This did not fit into my plan for encouraging productive risk-taking, so I bought myself some time. "Oh, Barbara," I said. "You're always thinking of others. I'm sure that we'd all benefit from learning more about digital writing assignments, but critical friends time was set aside so we'd have a safe place to ask questions about our work. Let's think more about this. Could we meet again tomorrow?"

We agreed to meet the next morning in the courtyard where we both had morning duty. I hoped we could have a substantive conversation while we supervised the dozens of students who congregated there each morning.

LOOKING FOR PATTERNS

Before we met, I once again examined the materials from our previous meetings and prayed for some insight. Two things popped out. First of all, Barbara's written reflections were full of evidence that, above all else, she valued a positive, warm atmosphere. Every month, she wrote things like, "I enjoy being part of a group and sharing" and, "I like discussing how work was successful." She had joined the group because she thought it might help the school recapture a feeling of community that she felt had been lost in recent years with various changes in leadership and personnel.

Barbara was a master at giving warm feedback, but the second thing I noticed was that she wrote *nothing* next to the "What didn't work" prompt for our first three meetings in the fall. I hadn't thought anything about the individual occurrences, but looking back at the reflections over time helped me see the pattern. I wondered if Barbara couldn't think of any advice to give me, or if she just felt uncomfortable delivering any kind of cool feedback.

In December, though, Barbara recorded her distress about Geraldine's laughing at Heather's presentation. After that meeting, she wrote, "I am puzzled about one person's actions as Heather presented. I am a very sensitive person, but I still felt the actions were not appropriate. I hope it didn't make Heather feel bad. The person may not realize how her actions are perceived."

Barbara could not speak ill of a colleague. She did not even refer to Geraldine by name. I was newly amazed at the energy that Barbara put into worrying about other people's feelings, but that gave me an idea of how to approach her.

DISCERNING THE QUESTION

Luckily, the weather was pleasant the next morning when we got together. We kept our eyes on the students as they milled about the courtyard, and I dove right into the preconference.

"Barbara, I went through all of our group's materials last night, and I want to start by saying how much I appreciate your contributions to our group. Your kindness and attention to people's feelings help us maintain a friendly atmosphere."

She beamed.

I continued, "Have you thought anymore about a question that you have? What concerns you? Do you wonder if you can do something better?"

"Well, I'd still like to help out by sharing what I know about digital writing assignments. Maybe the question could be, 'How can the teachers at Monroe improve student engagement in writing assignments?'"

"Barbara, do *you* teach writing? Are you really worried about writing objectives?"

"I care about everything that's taught here. But, you know, my role at this school keeps changing. I used to teach home economics, but that was phased out since it didn't fulfill any of the so-called standards. I saw the writing on the wall and got the skills I needed to teach computer science classes. I've done that for years, and this year the principal changed the schedule so that computer science is no longer a separate class. I just maintain the equipment, and the core teachers are supposed to integrate the technology lessons into their curriculum and come to the lab every once in a while to work on projects."

I could hear an undertone of frustration, so I pursued the topic. "How is that working out?"

"I hate it that I don't have my very own students. I don't feel like a teacher anymore. And most days, I feel like I have 80 bosses. Every teacher has a claim on my time. I hate to let people down, but it's very challenging to coordinate with everybody. I'm also worried that the students aren't getting enough exposure to the full range of technology objectives. Most teachers just use the lab for Internet research and word processing. There are a lot of missed opportunities."

"Barbara, that's your dilemma!"

"I don't see how it can help the group to listen to me complain about my job. We should all be thankful that we have a job."

"Okay, I know this is out of your comfort zone, but I think that your sharing your dilemma will be very helpful for our group. It's important for the new teachers to see that the veterans still take their jobs seriously. You are giving us the gift of your vulnerability, and using a protocol will keep it from devolving into a pity party. I know that you were upset by some comments at the December meeting, so I promise to facilitate it really strongly. I'll remind everybody of our feedback norms ahead of time instead of waiting for an infraction. You might even get some helpful feedback that would help you decide how to proceed with your new role."

"Okay, when you put it that way, how could I refuse? I will help the group by sharing my dilemma."

LESSONS LEARNED

Several possible focusing questions emerged, and we settled on, "How can I improve instructional coordination with the core teachers at Monroe?" By the end of the session, Barbara had several new ideas to try like asking to give mini-lessons about how to incorporate technology into the content areas during department meetings. She has already scheduled time with the English department to demonstrate strategies for digital writing assignments. She's also starting a blog that will raise awareness of the technology that's available and recognize teachers who are doing a good job with digital teaching.

Barbara was not the only beneficiary. During the debriefing, several group members talked about how taking on Barbara's dilemma helped them understand her role, and they now feel more comfortable approaching her with lessons that they would like to try out in the computer lab. Geraldine pointed out how the current course structure put low-income children at a disadvantage because they didn't always have access to technology at home and their access at school was now hit or miss without a dedicated class for learning technology objectives.

Finally, I learned that my group members have different motivations for being in the group and not everybody is seeking feedback. Some colleagues have to be encouraged to examine problems instead of just sharing successes. Also, from now on, I will not ask for volunteers to "present" their work for feedback. Instead, I'm going to emphasize the importance of questioning by dropping the term *presenter* and calling the person who brings in work the *chief inquirer*.

Chapter 3 Discussion Questions

What?

1. List the skills and facilitative strategies that Andrea uses throughout this case.
2. Andrea is a novice facilitator with just a few tools in her box. What other options would you suggest to her?

So What?

3. Andrea reflects on several months of meetings when she plans the next meeting. How does this long-range view affect her planning?
4. How does Andrea's friendship with Barbara help and/or hinder how Andrea approaches Barbara?

Now What?

5. What are the motivations and values of the people with whom you collaborate?

Becoming Listeners

> *Key Topics:* feedback norms; Zones of Comfort, Risk, and Danger; Collaborative Assessment Conference; resistance; Success Analysis Protocol for Individuals
>
> *Key Challenges:* using unfamiliar protocols, responding to resistance to protocols

CONTEXT

A novice critical friends group coach at Monroe Middle School, Andrea depends on protocols to help her group have conversations that are focused on teaching and learning. Protocols are agreed-upon structures for conversation that build in time and space for questioning, listening, responding, and reflecting.

During her initial CFG training, Andrea learned and practiced basic protocols such as the Consultancy and Tuning protocols. Now, several months into her first year of leading this group of teaching colleagues, Andrea has begun to explore the School Reform Initiative's website and other resources to search for additional protocols to use with her group.

Because she appreciates the protocols so much, Andrea is surprised when some colleagues resist using them. How can Andrea respond to this resistance and continue to use protocols to guide and enrich the group's professional conversations?

ANDREA SPEAKS ABOUT USING PROTOCOLS

A hallmark of our critical friends group training last summer was learning how to use protocols to have professional conversations, and I love protocols because they help me be an effective facilitator. Some teachers ask why we can't be trusted to simply talk about our professional practice. I'll tell you why: Those unfacilitated conversations would stray all over the place. At least, that's what happens in the faculty lounge where we go to vent, commiserate, cheer one another up, and maybe get some informal advice. It's also where we talk about which websites have the best shoe sales and how horribly our local sports teams have been playing. In contrast, the CFG is a time and place set aside for professional learning from peers, and I appreciate how the protocols help our group stay on topic.

I also appreciate how using protocols helps us be good stewards of our time together. Our monthly after-school CFG meetings are just 2 hours long. With 15 minutes at the beginning for signing in, passing around the snacks, and Connections (Thompson-Grove, cited in School Reform Initiative, 2014)—a contemplative activity that prepares our minds for the meeting— and then 15 minutes at the end for debriefing and writing reflections, we have just an hour and a half to get some serious work done. With careful attention to the time frames, we can use protocols to do two complete look- ing at work sessions or have time to both discuss an article and explore a teaching dilemma.

Finally, I am thankful that protocols lend me some extra authority. They help us take turns, balance our voices, and attend to different types of ques- tions. Protocols also allow for quiet time. I especially like the way they give me, a young coach, permission to remind some group members that it's time for questions instead of advice or that it's time to listen instead of speak.

The feedback I get about protocols is somewhat mixed. Some partic- ipants have said that the conversations are "stiff" or "awkward," but one of Geraldine's written reflections summed it up nicely: "I've learned to talk less and listen more. Andrea's leadership keeps us focused and on task in order to use our time wisely."

I'm proud of the way my group has jumped right in to look at student work each month. One of the other three CFGs at Monroe Middle School is still "building trust" by doing team builders and reading articles before they use protocols to learn from student work and dilemmas. My group is build- ing trust by actually doing the hard work of giving and receiving feedback.

LAYING THE GROUNDWORK

One of the reasons our group has shared work successfully is that we laid the groundwork in our early meetings. (See Chapters 2 and 3 for more details about this group's earlier meetings.)

Setting Feedback Norms

Back in September, we set a respectful tone by talking about the conditions we need to do our best work and agreeing on meeting norms that we review at the beginning of each meeting. In October, before any of us presented our students' work, we did the Feedback Nightmares activity (Mohr, cited in School Reform Initiative, 2014), in which we each journaled about times when we had bad experiences giving and receiving feedback. After writing about our experiences, we shared our stories with partners, pulled out the commonalities, and made a list of feedback dos and don'ts. The partners shared our lists with the whole group and we edited our feedback norms to be:

- Start with the positive.
- Support one another with sensitive comments.
- Use discretion.
- Base feedback on observable facts.
- Give feedback only when asked.
- Be honest.
- Be professional.

Some of these items are in tension with one another. For example, I wondered how we could agree to both "give feedback only when asked" and "be honest." To follow these norms, we would have to cultivate good judgment and continue to trust one another.

Zones of Comfort, Risk, and Danger

Another piece of groundwork that I purposefully placed on an agenda was the Zones of Comfort, Risk, and Danger activity (School Reform Initiative, 2014). During this activity, we had a conversation about how the same experience might be risky for one teacher, comfortable for another, and feel dangerous for a third. We touched on some things that sent us into the danger zone, such as unproductive conflict, feeling like confidentiality might be breached, and talking about somewhat taboo topics on our campus such as how race, ethnicity, and class might affect someone's experience at Monroe Middle School.

I emphasized how the zone of risk is often where the most powerful learning takes place and we should feel comfortable being vulnerable with one another because the protocols were designed to help us stay out of the danger zone. As I learned in my CFG training, protocols "constrain behavior in order to enhance experience" (McDonald et al., 2007, p. 8).

CHOOSING THE BEST PROTOCOL

Throughout the fall, we used the Tuning and Consultancy protocols to look at work, but neither seemed appropriate for what Geraldine wanted to bring to the table in February. At our preconference, it sounded like she didn't really have a question, but she was desperate for some fresh perspective.

For the first couple of decades of her teaching career, Geraldine had taught in schools with predominantly African American students and teachers. Because she had earned a reputation in regional social studies professional organizations as a teacher who maintained high standards for all students, the social studies department chair at Monroe Middle School had wooed her into joining our campus, which had a quite diverse student body and staff.

For years, Geraldine had been a master at using the community to support her students, but she didn't have the same deep ties to the community surrounding Monroe that she had had at her previous school. For the first time in her long career, Geraldine's classes included many immigrant students who did not yet speak English, and Geraldine was flummoxed by how to reach out to them and their families. Strategies such as talking to students' parents and grandparents when she saw them around the neighborhood, or reaching out to pastors at the nearby churches, just weren't possible anymore, and Geraldine couldn't make sense of the work some kids were turning in.

I decided to try using the Collaborative Assessment Conference (Blythe, Allen, & Powell, 2008) to help us suspend judgment, look carefully and closely at what was actually there, and broaden our perspectives.

ENGAGING IN A COLLABORATIVE ASSESSMENT CONFERENCE

When I explained how the Collaborative Assessment Conference worked, Geraldine was intrigued and agreed to bring several samples of one student's work for us to examine at the next CFG meeting.

I was a little worried about facilitating a protocol that was mostly unfamiliar to me. I had seen it used once in a small group at a professional development conference, but hadn't gotten to practice it myself. The Collaborative Assessment Conference is different from the protocols that I had used previously because the presenter provides neither context for the work nor a framing question. Participants have to be skilled at describing the work in front of them without judging it. As the facilitator, I would have to pay close attention to each statement and intervene when anyone in the group strayed from the protocol's steps.

When the February meeting rolled around, we practiced telling the difference between descriptive, interpretive, and evaluative statements before we dove into the actual Collaborative Assessment Conference. When I thought we were ready to move forward, Geraldine reached into her bag and brought out a stack of work that she had collected from one student over the past few weeks.

We all knew that Geraldine taught U.S. history, but she didn't tell us anything else about the student, the assignments, or her expectations. The 10 of us silently examined the work, passed it around, and took notes about what we saw.

While Geraldine listened, the rest of us engaged in a series of rounds. At first, I asked, "What do you see?" and we really delved into details. I occasionally had to redirect an evaluative comment, such as when Heather said, "All the responses on this worksheet are too short" instead of something purely descriptive like "The response to question #6 has three words."

During the next two rounds, we responded to the prompts, "What questions does this work raise for you?" and "What do you think the child is working on?" After the rounds, Geraldine had a chance to provide her own perspective about the student's work and let us know if any of our comments were surprising or unexpected. Finally, together we discussed the implications for teaching and learning. Having a heterogeneous group was really an asset at this time. Unlike at a department meeting where Geraldine could interact with only other social studies teachers, the makeup of our CFG allowed her to connect with teachers from many departments. Both Joyce, the ESL teacher, and Carlos, the Spanish teacher, had surmised that the student was a native Spanish speaker and had specific advice about how to support the student, and Wanda, the speech therapist, shared her expertise about language acquisition and development. I was impressed by the group's collective knowledge.

In our oral debriefing after the protocol, the general consensus was that participating in the Collaborative Assessment Conference had helped all of us see the challenges of teaching English language learners in a new light. Although we were able to come up with a list of possible strategies that Geraldine could use to support her students, the true value of the Collaborative Assessment Conference was in enhancing our observation skills. We were becoming better listeners, and Geraldine felt more confident and energized about modifying her practice to meet her new teaching context.

ARTICULATING RESISTANCE TO PROTOCOLS

Carlos's reflection perfectly summed up the value of the Collaborative Assessment Conference for our group:

The activities we did today helped me think about deeper questions. I realized that protocols are not about finding a quick fix to your problem. Instead of a solution, the presenter can walk away with questions to think about over time in order to come to a deeper understanding of the issue and possible actions to take.

Because I agreed with Carlos and felt like the group had had a rich experience that evening, I was shocked to read that Lori, the new math teacher on campus, had filled her entire reflection sheet with a heartfelt critique of protocols:

I don't like the protocols. I feel like there is an opportunity to come here and walk away from great discussions that help us redesign how our class looks and runs, or discussions that challenge everyone, not just the presenter, to be a better teacher. I don't feel like that's happening. I personally am uncomfortable with the protocols and feel limited by their strict guidelines. I want to brainstorm; I want to problem solve with this group of "friends," all of whom are working toward the same greater goal. Do we have to do protocols every time? Can we get in groups and discuss without parameters? I don't think safety is a concern with our small group. I'd like to explore ways in which we can share what's worked for us in support of bettering someone else—without having to phrase it in a particular way.

Lori had packed a lot of frustration into that one-page reflection sheet. She was obviously uncomfortable with what she perceived as "strict guidelines" and seemed to assume that the discussions benefitted only the presenter instead of offering insights to all of the participants.

She also seemed to value the "problem-solving" aspects of our work together to the exclusion of other goals such as broadening our professional understanding. I wondered if Lori was even listening to the entire conversation.

WONDERINGS

I wondered if Lori's resistance, especially her desire for more explicit problem solving during our meetings, was related to her being a math teacher. Does a teacher's subject area influence how they react to protocols? I couldn't tell for sure, because Lori was the only math teacher in our motley group, but I had noticed that Tracy, the English teacher in our CFG, could usually immediately make connections between the protocols we used in our CFG meetings and her own classroom practice. Tracy had already tried using some protocols with her students to look at texts more critically and to fine-tune writing assignments.

I also wondered if the way I introduced protocols to our CFG last fall had focused so much on how protocols promote safe conversations that other understandings had been excluded in Lori's mind. Yet, other members had made meaning of the protocol experience in a variety of ways over the first several months that we met. The italicized words in the following examples highlight the different ways that members conceptualized protocols. For example, Barbara wrote that protocols were "*tools* for developing as professionals." Carlos imagined protocols as machines that produced "positive *output* in discussion."

Several members thought of protocols as glasses or hearing aids that enhanced our professional senses. Joyce wrote, "The Collaborative Assessment Conference allowed Geraldine to *hear and see* the sophistication of the student's work," and back in the fall, Wanda had shared, "I absolutely loved the protocols we used tonight; they really *opened my eyes* to how a helpful conversation should work."

Like Lori, Heather seemed to conceptualize protocols as barriers, but she expressed a much more positive feeling about the protocols' constraints when she wrote last fall, "I like the clarifying questioning component because the speaker is *limited* in their response and it *forces the participants* to stay on topic." No single concept was adequate for understanding the use of protocols.

Finally, I wondered if I could understand and address Lori's resistance better if I got to know her better. Because Lori teaches 8th-grade math and her classroom is out in the trailers by the athletic fields, I hardly ever casually run into her on campus, and we never attend any of the same department or grade-level meetings. I realized that I didn't know her very well.

CHANGING MY COACHING PRACTICE

I wasn't willing to back down from using protocols just to make one group member feel more comfortable. I decided to try a multipronged approach. First, I would try to have a looser demeanor when facilitating protocols. Instead of abruptly quitting a section when time had run out, I would try to be smoother and more subtle when transitioning from one part of a protocol to another. Second, before the end of the year, I would try to craft an agenda that took Lori's specific needs into account.

Success Analysis Protocol for Individuals

In March, we dedicated the entire meeting to an activity called Success Analysis Protocol for Individuals (School Reform Initiative, 2014). We split into triads and each person wrote a short description of one best practice of their work within the past year and also jotted down what made that work different from other experiences. After one person in a triad shared his or her best practice and what made it different, the other two would analyze what they heard and offer additional insights. The members rotated facilitation and timekeeping duties, and the process allowed for more interaction. At the end of the meeting, all of us gathered to talk about the traits that made our best work stand out. It was a great way to reconnect with our teaching values and celebrate successes as we approached the onslaught of springtime standardized testing.

Lori had a much more positive attitude with this flexible format. She wrote, "I enjoyed the fluidity of the process today. I felt like our group was able to discuss our successes freely while asking questions to learn from each other's accomplishments. I appreciated the informal structure of the discussion and the comfort it initiated."

Learning from Presenting

Because I wanted to build on Lori's emerging positive attitude, I encouraged her to bring work to our April meeting. When I walked out to her trailer for the preconference, Lori explained that she wanted the CFG to give her advice and new strategies to use during the Saturday math tutorials that had been mandated for students who were in danger of failing the state tests.

"Lori," I pointed out, "nobody else in our group is a math teacher. Wouldn't your math department chair be a better resource for specific instructional strategies?"

"Andrea, ever since I was nominated for Rookie of the Year, the math department has been teasing me. I don't want them to know that I need help with planning the tutorials."

"Oh, wow, that puts a different spin on things," I responded. "You've mentioned that the constraints in the protocols make you uncomfortable. Part of my job as a facilitator is to make sure that you don't get into the danger zone, but I want to make sure that we are all learning. Would it be too much of a risk to try this process called Peeling the Onion (School Reform Initiative, 2014)? You'll have to do a lot of listening, but it can help us get a more robust picture of your problem before we jump in and try to solve it."

"I'll give it a try, Andrea. But I really want to know what to do on Saturday morning!"

LEARNING FROM LISTENING

At the April meeting, Lori described her dilemma and then listened while the group proceeded through a series of rounds that surfaced assumptions and raised questions. Only after going through these rounds did we talk about options for improving Lori's tutorial activities. Her reflection sheet from that meeting had a much more positive tone. She wrote:

> I really enjoyed tonight. I really liked my protocol: Peeling the Onion. I feel much better after reflecting on the tutorial process and hearing the rest of my group's thoughts. I feel really challenged to be a better teacher after tonight. I want to go home and really plan out what/how I can do for my kids—after being prompted by my group.

Lori remained focused on making concrete plans, but it seemed that she was beginning to appreciate how Peeling the Onion brought different voices to bear on her issue and gave her ideas for a more robust plan of action.

Chapter 4 Discussion Questions

What?

1. What is a protocol?
2. How are protocols used to enhance professional development in a group setting?

So What?

3. Can a professional development group call itself a critical friends group if it does not regularly use protocols?
4. What groups (besides CFGs) could benefit from using protocols?
5. Why might some educators resist using protocols?

Now What?

6. What images do you use to understand how protocols work?
7. Where can you go to learn about new protocols or practice using them?

Building Relationships for Sustainability

Healthy professional relationships support effective collaboration in schools, and the three scenarios of Part II feature facilitators who persevere with their colleagues even when their relationships are floundering. In Chapter 5, "Engaging a Reluctant Team Member," a participant who is always tardy to meetings and disengaged even when he is present frustrates Elnara, a facilitator who supports a group of early-career teachers. Chapter 6, "Dealing with Difficult People," features the voice of a parent leader, Darlene, whose patience is tried by another involved parent. Chapter 7, "Navigating Conflict," delves into the practice of Juling, a consultant who must help a team of curriculum leaders overcome the interpersonal impediments to their team development.

Engaging a Reluctant Team Member

> *Key Topics:* disengaged adult learners, Peeling the Onion
>
> *Key Challenges:* building healthy professional relationships, intervening with adult learners

CONTEXT

Elnara and Toni are experienced teachers who co-coach a learning community comprised of 14 second-year teachers who work in several different schools across the region. The school district established learning communities of new teachers like this one in order to give novice teachers the support and encouragement they need to thrive in the classroom. Although participation in the group is voluntary, the participants commit to being in a group for 2 years, and they get a small stipend for completing a year's worth of meetings.

At an organizational meeting held at the beginning of the semester, the members agreed to meet at a centrally located high school on the first Monday of each month from 5:30 to 8:30 p.m., but Andre and Jen, two coworkers who carpool together, are always late. Andre seems especially disconnected from all the other group members, and his disengagement has become a distraction to the other teachers. After a few months of struggling with this reluctant group member, Elnara and Toni feel stymied and want help thinking of ways to work through this problem.

ELNARA DESCRIBES ANDRE'S DISENGAGEMENT

Toni and I have a learning community member whose behavior and attitude really put a damper on our monthly meetings. I dread having to interact with Andre, and I am frustrated that I haven't been able to establish a healthy working relationship with him. Here are some of the behaviors that get on my nerves. He and the friend that he carpools with always show up at least 10 minutes late, and he usually has a blank expression on his face. Andre keeps his cell phone out all the time, and it looks like he texts during meetings. He hardly interacts with anybody in the group except for Jen because they happen to teach at the same school and drive to our meetings together.

Because they are always late to our monthly meetings, Andre and Jen usually miss most of the get-to-know-you activities that we've planned, but a few weeks ago, Toni and I scheduled the Warp Speed (School Reform Initiative, 2014) activity in the middle of the agenda to act as an energizer as well as an icebreaker. This activity involves tossing a ball to another group member while you say their name. After I set up the activity, Andre flatly stated, "I don't know anybody's name," as if that were a good excuse for not participating.

On the inside, I was seething: "Really?! A grown man doesn't care enough to learn just one person's name?" On the outside, I think I said something neutral like, "Well, this is Becky from Willow High School. You can toss the ball to her."

Besides missing out on the team-building aspects of our group, Andre also expresses disdain for protocols. In an early reflection, he wrote, "Waiting for answers didn't work for me. It caused a bit of inefficient time usage." At another meeting when we broke into triads to share stories for the Success Analysis Protocol for Individuals (School Reform Initiative, 2014), his group finished before any of the others. As I circulated among the groups, I noticed that they didn't use all the allotted time for asking clarifying questions and really delving into one another's stories. There's a clear pattern in his reflections of indicating that he thinks the main purpose of the protocols is simply to protect the presenter from harsh feedback, and he prefers a more "feisty back-and-forth" communication style. I'm putting words in his mouth now, but it's like he thinks protocols are for sissies who can't handle criticism. He doesn't grasp the need to take a few minutes to make sure you understand the problem before you attempt to solve it.

It also ticks me off that his written reflections are often shallow and trite. He'll include comments like, "I'm happy I got a free composition book" or "More pink candy would be spectacular." Most important, whenever he's in a small group with Jen, she also says she dislikes protocols, but when Toni and I surreptitiously break them up, she'll participate more fully and make insightful comments. I feel like Andre is dragging all of us down and that I'm a failure as a facilitator when it comes to establishing a healthy group climate to help us do our work.

GETTING PEER FEEDBACK

Luckily for me, all the coaches of these new-teacher learning communities meet once a month to share dinner and some professional discussion. This monthly dinner was the perfect venue for Toni and me to get feedback about our coaching dilemma.

Presenting the Problem

One of our colleagues offered to facilitate a Peeling the Onion (School Reform Initiative, 2014) protocol for us. During the first step, I described my frustration with Andre and added some of my own reflections about why Toni and I were having such a hard time reaching him. For starters, unlike the school-based groups that I used to coach, the members of these multischool learning communities don't see one another except at their monthly meeting, so it's more of a challenge to bond and truly care about one another's work. Also, Andre did not attend the organizational meeting at the beginning of the year, so he missed the conversations about how these groups are supposed to act like personalized professional development in which everybody will have a chance to get feedback, and he had no direct input about the time and place for our monthly meetings. I also remember that he left our very first group meeting early because he had a runny nose and a sore throat. I wonder if I was too soft on him when I encouraged him to go home and rest—maybe I inadvertently sent a message that it doesn't matter if he is there or not. I'm also distressed that because he and Jen are always late, there is no time for the informal connecting that often builds relationships and smooths interactions. Finally, I also wonder if race, gender, and age are barriers to communication. Andre is a young Black man, and both Toni and I are middle-aged White women. Mainly, I feel like we already have a broken relationship and that there is no time to fix it before the end of the year.

During the Peeling the Onion protocol, I also shared some strategies that Toni and I have tried such as reading the written reflections from the previous meeting aloud at the beginning of each meeting to show that all voices are valued. We also include time for debriefing protocols and getting other participants to say what they value about the meetings and the structures that we use. Of course, we also review the norms that the group developed about participation and engagement, but if Andre and his friend are really late, they miss the review. So my questions are:

- How do you build a healthy working relationship with somebody that you see for just 2 or 3 hours a month?
- What strategies do you use to encourage reluctant adults?
- How do you influence an adult's behavior in a way that keeps everybody's dignity intact?

Active Listening

After I described our dilemma and asked the focusing questions, the coaches' group asked some informational clarifying questions, and we then moved into a series of rounds during which Toni and I listened and took notes while our colleagues responded to these prompts:

- "What I heard Elnara say is . . ."
- "One assumption that seems to be part of the problem is . . ." or "One thing I assume to be true about this problem is . . ."
- "A question this raises for me is . . ."
- "Further questions this raises for me are . . ."
- "What if . . . ?" or "Have we thought about . . . ?" or "I wonder. . . ."

I truly love the part of the protocol where my colleagues went through several rounds of what they heard me say. They definitely heard that I was frustrated and they picked up on the fact that I had not directly told Andre how frustrated I am. They also heard me say that he negatively impacts people in our group, and that I am sorry we have such a broken relationship.

Raising Assumptions

Over the years, I've found that the round where the protocol participants voice their assumptions is especially challenging. It seems that people don't really know what an assumption is—a statement that is simply accepted or supposed to be true without proof. Discussing assumptions seems more personal than other steps because it is impossible to discuss assumptions without laying bare our own values. However, my colleagues did a fine job. Here are some of the assumptions that they voiced:

I [the other coaches] assume that . . .
. . . the facilitators want to rectify this relationship.
. . . successful teachers are willing to dig deeper into protocols.
. . . Andre feels like his attendance is mandatory.

. . . the facilitators feel disrespected.

. . . others in the group are being disrespected.

. . . Andre knows there is a problem.

. . . he doesn't think he'll be confronted.

. . . the facilitators don't think they'd be received well.

. . . he doesn't feel attached to the group.

. . . there's no reason for him to change his behavior.

. . . if he were not part of the group, it would thrive.

Expanding the Questions

Here's a sample of the comments I jotted down during the next few rounds of lifting-up questions:

A question this raises for me is . . .

. . . why does he act like this?

. . . if he holds back adults, what is he doing to kids?

. . . if he's absent, how will things change?

. . . how would he respond to direct confrontation?

. . . what would his response be if a student acted like that?

. . . why does the coworker feel free to participate when not in the same group as Andre?

After the rounds of Peeling the Onion, I got to review my notes and reflect out loud about what I was learning. In this particular case, I felt like my critical friends were voicing what I already knew to be true. I knew that I needed to talk to Andre and let him know that I was disappointed in his tardiness and his resistance to the group's activities, but I hate confronting adults. Hearing my colleagues also brought forward the fact that Andre's disengagement and my own reluctance to deal with it was negatively impacting the whole group. If I let things continue as they were, I might lose the entire group. Peeling the Onion helped me figure out the deep-seated tension I felt between needing to use my authority as a coach and wanting to just ignore the problem and hope it would resolve itself.

During the *Now What?* section of the protocol, we talked about ways to rebuild my relationship with Andre. Even though he didn't seem to value protocols, Toni and I had already gotten him to agree to present work at an upcoming meeting. It was my custom to hold preconferences with this group over the telephone and over email, but for him, I decided that only an in-person conference would do.

MAKING A CHANGE

I arranged to go to his school one afternoon so I could visit with him on his own turf. After I signed in at his high school's main office, Andre walked with me through the hallways and showed me his classroom. Just by looking at how he arranged the furniture and organized his classroom, I could tell that he works hard to differentiate instruction for his students. Sure enough, the problem that Andre wanted to bring to the group was about how to maximize the effectiveness of a tutoring program by differentiating it for various students.

As we conversed about his work during the preconference, I got a more complete picture of what Andre is like as a teacher and as a person. For example, I decided that I shouldn't take his blank expressions and propensity for texting personally: He was like that with everybody—even when his assistant principal stopped by to introduce herself.

Also, I had assumed that Andre's tardiness to our monthly meetings was entirely his fault, but I found out that his carpool partner was actually the one who habitually left late for meetings because she also coached a sports team. It was quite humbling for me to have several assumptions shattered when we had our one-on-one meeting.

That meeting was a breakthrough moment for Andre and me, and he has been more engaged since I went to his school. At the next learning community meeting, we tuned his proposal about the differentiated tutoring program, and he responded more thoughtfully to other participants. A month later, he reflected, "I normally am not a fan of protocols, but I really invested in J. T.'s presentation because I had the exact same problem," so at least he is finally connecting with some other group members. He even called me at home a few weeks ago to let me know ahead of time that he would have to miss a meeting for a family emergency. Andre may never be a big fan of collaborative work, and I think that he is naturally reserved instead of happily interactive, but I'm glad that we didn't give up on each other.

Chapter 5 Discussion Questions

What?

1. List the skills and facilitative strategies that Elnara used throughout this scenario.

So What?

2. Which strategies worked? Which were ineffective?
3. What are some other options that Elnara and Toni could have considered?

Now What?

4. Have you ever been in a similar situation? What did you do? What do you wish you had done?
5. Do you think participation in groups such as critical friends groups should be voluntary or mandatory?
6. How much tension can a group tolerate?

Dealing with Difficult People

> *Key Topics:* parent involvement, volunteer organizations, team building, financial accountability, Compass Points protocol
>
> *Key Challenges*: managing conflict, personalizing responses

CONTEXT

An experienced counselor at a suburban elementary school, Darlene is also an active volunteer and president of the Peerless Panther Band Boosters, a parent organization that supports the wind and percussion programs at North Pointe High School where her oldest son plays the trumpet.

Last year, the nominating committee reached out to Darlene and asked her to run for president of the Band Boosters because they thought she had the organizational experience and calm disposition needed to get the group refocused and re-energized. They were concerned that previous boards had sown the seeds of cliquishness through poor communication and lack of transparency and that fewer parents were volunteering for fundraisers and other projects that helped the band excel. Darlene agreed to serve as president and felt that she had a mandate to focus on building community and getting the organizational house in order.

Even though she has professional experience with helping children develop positive peer relationships and reduce conflict, Darlene's ability to manage conflict is stretched to the limit by some of the other adult volunteers. What can Darlene do to keep this organization on track?

DARLENE SPEAKS ABOUT HER EXPERIENCE

North Pointe High School has a long tradition of excellence in the fine arts. I should know because I myself played snare drum in the award-winning North

Pointe Peerless Panther Drum Corps almost 30 years ago. Besides a strong marching band, the program includes symphonic bands, a jazz ensemble, and even a mariachi band.

In the current age of government budget cuts, this ongoing dedication to music education would be impossible without the involvement of parents, and I'm the current president of the Band Boosters at my child's high school. The Peerless Panther Band Boosters is a 501(c)(3) nonprofit organization with a three-part mission to raise funds for the band, build community among band families, and support all aspects of the band programming.

I think that the nominating committee did a fantastic job of putting a slate of nominees together for this year's board. Besides a president, secretary, and treasurer, there are four vice presidents who each lead a set of related committees. The first VP, Daryl, is in charge of all the fundraising committees, and the second VP coordinates the social activities and improves communication through our e-newsletters and website. The third and fourth VPs share responsibility for the many support committees, such as for travel, uniforms, and equipment.

DARLENE'S LEADERSHIP PHILOSOPHY

My philosophy of being president is that it's my job to keep track of the big picture and create an atmosphere where people *want* to be involved. I'm a stickler about keeping an accurate calendar, but I don't need my hands in every little thing that the Band Boosters have taken on. The current vice presidents are all so smart and experienced that I feel confident about delegating. In fact, I served on the board as secretary last year, and one of my pet peeves was watching last year's VPs ask people to serve on a committee or be a committee chair and then micromanage everything. The way I see it, the board's job is to create policy and then let the worker bees have their say and do all the work.

I drew on my skills as a counselor and facilitative leader to work with the board over the summer. At our very first meeting, I facilitated an icebreaker called 3-2-1. Each person jotted down 3 things about themselves, 2 things that they love about the Peerless Panther Band, and 1 burning question that they had about the Band Boosters. As we shared our answers, we learned about one another and our values. The burning questions included a range of concerns such as why fewer parents are volunteering, whether we could have a relaxed event like a family picnic, what projects need money, and what role the board plays. We all agreed that our number-one goal was to improve the sense of community of the Band Boosters, and we even talked about how all initiatives could be team-building experiences. Instead of evaluating the Boosters' success with only simplistic measures such as how much money we raised, we decided to also keep track of the number of first-time volunteers and total number of volunteer hours and conduct a parent survey at some time during the year to ask for direct feedback.

INTRODUCING DARYL

One of the newcomers on the board is Daryl. He is the vice president for fundraising, and I really appreciate his work ethic. He is present at every meeting and is amazingly organized. His twin boys are sophomores this year, but when they were freshmen, Daryl and his wife volunteered wherever they could. Daryl's major contribution has been getting the dads organized to load and unload equipment for all the football games, contests, and concerts. Although I think of myself as a feminist, I appreciate how having more dads involved at the school is really an asset, and Daryl has encouraged dozens more dads to get involved in the Band Boosters instead of sitting on the sidelines and letting the moms do all the actual work.

Daryl sees it as his personal mission to keep the facilities in good shape. He is very handy, and after a serious rainstorm flooded the practice fields and the parking lot where the marching band learns its formations, Daryl and his sons cleaned up all the accumulated mud with shovels, brooms, and a power washer before the band directors even thought to ask somebody to do it.

I also appreciate the fact that Daryl is a sharp businessman, and he used his negotiating skills to get the Band Boosters much better deals with the various vendors we use for fundraisers.

THE CLASH

As much as I appreciate Daryl's "just get it done" attitude, I think that he is the most annoying person on the board. For example, early last fall, the board voted to spend up to $1,000 to purchase materials to improve the storage closets where all the uniforms are stored. Daryl offered to use his handyman skills to add as much shelving as possible and upgrade the lighting so we can actually see everything that's in the closet. Although we went ahead and committed the funds, I thought we had an understanding that the actual work could be completed later in the year when marching season was over and our schedules weren't so busy with weekly football games and traveling to marching contests.

Daryl had a different idea. He wanted to jump right in and get it done. The morning after the meeting, Daryl sent an email to Jenny, the Booster treasurer, and cc'd me. He asked for immediate access to the funds and suggested that Jenny obtain a prepaid credit card so that Daryl could go to the lumber store to get the materials. Jenny wrote back that evening when she got home from work and explained that getting a prepaid credit card was not the best way to account for the money. She suggested that Daryl go to the lumber store and get a statement for how much the shelving and fixtures would cost. Jenny could then write a check to the store ahead of time for the exact amount, or Daryl could pay for the items himself and she would write a reimbursement check as soon as possible. She also gave us a heads up that she would soon be on an extended business trip, and she felt stretched thin because one of her younger children had been ill. She and her husband were doing a juggling act to keep their two jobs and family obligations in balance. Understandably, Jenny's volunteer work was at the bottom of her priority list.

Because Jenny was an experienced treasurer, I deferred to her judgment about how the purchases should be made and recorded. I'm no accountant, but I know that maintaining impeccable financial records is mandatory for keeping our tax-exempt status. I don't want to end up owing back taxes and fines if the Band Boosters are ever audited. When it comes to finances, I prefer being slow and careful. The shelves could wait.

Daryl was ticked off. On top of that, another crisis emerged when the third VP and the committee chair in charge of travel arrangements got into an argument and the committee chair resigned. This was a huge blow because the band was traveling to the state capital in less than a month's time. I talked to each woman one-on-one, but the damage had already been done. Other members stepped up to get the work done, but I was getting more and more resentful of these unexpected demands on my time. Although I'm dedicated to running the Band Boosters in a professional way, it is a volunteer organization. We need to put the egos aside and be kind to one another.

It was quite clear that the board needed to do some work around our work styles and exactly what we could expect from one another as the leaders.

ADDRESSING THE TENSIONS

I was afraid that this tension would eat up all the good feelings that we had worked so hard to establish over the summer. I sent this email to the entire board.

Dear Board Members:

Several people have expressed frustration with issues such as feeling ignored or undervalued, feeling stymied, feeling overwhelmed, and feeling unsure about proper procedures.

I strongly believe that working through this must be done **face-to-face**. The first item on the Board Meeting Agenda for our next regular meeting will be discussing and negotiating the expectations that we have of one another as well as guidelines for communicating effectively. If this is the only thing we do that evening, it will be time well spent.

I have been so impressed and amazed at what we've been able to accomplish so far as an all-volunteer organization. I hope this can make us be even more effective.

> Most sincerely,
> Darlene
> Peerless Panther Band
> Booster President

I drew on my experiences as a counselor to develop an agenda for that evening and decided to do the Compass Points (School Reform Initiative, 2014) protocol as an activity to help us understand our preferences in group work. In the Compass Points protocol, each direction represents a particular work style. For example, a "North" is someone who likes to act and plunge right in. A "West" pays attention to detail and asks a lot of questions before acting. An "East" likes to look at the big picture and the possibilities before acting, and a "South" is very caring and likes to know that everyone's feelings have been taken into consideration and that their voices have been heard. After the facilitator reads a description of the four directions out loud, each member self-selects what direction he or she is. They get with the other people who share that direction, answer some reflective questions about the strengths and limitations of their style, and present the answers to the whole group. When the activity goes well, the participants gain insight into their own style and learn what other people need in order to work together effectively.

It was easy to peg Daryl as a North—someone who jumps right in and gets things done. I wanted the whole board to be aware of our different personality types and appreciate how we each bring something important to the team. I especially wanted Daryl to see that I admired his talent for starting and completing initiatives, but the organization had to balance that with attention to detail, regard for feelings, and a clear focus on our overarching mission.

FROM BAD TO WORSE

The activity was a disaster. We hold our meetings in a classroom near the band hall, and Daryl actually walked out of the room. He stood in the hall and pretended to make phone calls for work while the rest of us engaged in the activity.

I didn't know what to do. Should I publicly berate him? If I were really his boss, I would have written him up for undermining my authority, but I was afraid that Daryl might resign in disgust if I confronted him. Would confronting Daryl get the group back on track or make it disintegrate?

I struggled internally. Should I do nothing and just go on with the activity? I really wanted to see how the other board members self-identified, but what I really, really wanted was for Daryl to pay attention. I wanted to be respected and appreciated for what I bring to the table. I wanted Daryl to respect the *team*, but he was pouting out in the hall. At that moment, I felt desperate for an outside facilitator. Taking care of the agenda, taking care of our learning, taking care of Daryl, and taking care of myself was too much for one person.

I remembered reading an article called "The Zen of Facilitation" (Killion & Simmons, 1992) that advised, "If unsure what to do, do nothing," so I slogged through the activity as planned and let Daryl stew by himself out in the hall. The rest of us learned that the second VP and I are Easts. Our detail-oriented treasurer is definitely a West, and the rest of the VPs are Norths—although some said they had trouble deciding and could have stood in another group. Only our secretary, Lois, was a South who prioritized hearing all voices. My vision of a highly functioning board focused on community building was crumbling around me.

EVEN MORE AWKWARDNESS

I delayed dealing with Daryl and busied myself with making sure that the trip to the capital went as planned. A few weeks after the Compass Points incident, Daryl and I found ourselves working side by side selling tickets to the holiday dance in the cafeteria. Our conversation was cordial, so I felt like the tensions from the previous board meeting had been smoothed over. Perhaps time does heal all wounds.

When I gathered my things and headed out to the parking lot to return to my job for the afternoon, Daryl was close behind. "Hey, Darlene," he called out. "Can I talk to you about something?"

I smiled and thought to myself, "Nice. He's finally going to apologize for walking out of the board meeting."

Daryl held the lobby door open for me and when we got outside he said, "I didn't want to embarrass you in front of the board, so I've been wanting to catch you alone. I think you play around too much during our meetings."

I was flabbergasted. I was expecting an apology, and instead I got a dressing-down about how my vision—which I thought was a shared vision with the whole board—was inadequate and my concerns about process were just a waste of time.

Daryl's vision was all about making physical improvements to the band facilities and equipment. If anybody had questions, they were just being obstructionist. He thought that I should toughen up and make Jenny, the treasurer, do all of her tasks in a more timely manner. And instead of having an icebreaker or team builder at each meeting, we should just stick to business.

I wilted. I felt like we had no common ground. What others thought were my best leadership qualities—an ability to bring people together, the skills to run interactive meetings, a value for listening to multiple perspectives—Daryl thought were my deficiencies. I felt totally inadequate. Daryl needed a president with a different set of leadership qualities. How could I possibly be what I considered to be my best self and run the Band Boosters in a way that Daryl could respect?

MAKING A RECOVERY

I had obviously lost a lot of credibility with Daryl, so I tried to calm down and use this tête-à-tête to repair our relationship. First, I just listened as he unloaded all the ways that he was concerned with the progress of the Band Boosters. I tried to project a neutral stance and show concern for Daryl's perspective and his frustration. I didn't want to start an argument. I just wanted to listen and understand.

As he talked, I realized that Daryl and his energy were misplaced on the board. Instead of fundraising, he should have been in charge of all the facilities and the never-ending efforts to keep the uniforms clean and the equipment in good repair. He was happiest when his hands were busy and his task was clear. Flexibility and ambiguity agitated him.

However, when he started to reiterate that I needed to toughen up and give more directives to the other officers, I decided that I needed to toughen up with him.

"Daryl," I interrupted. "I'm hearing you say that we need clear lines of authority, so I'm wondering why you walked out of the board meeting last month. I'm the president, and I felt disrespected when you refused to participate."

He looked sheepish. "Well, I hadn't thought of it that way. I didn't see the point of doing an activity where you already knew the answers. You said yourself that you knew I was a North, or whatever."

"I know, Daryl. I tried to create a learning experience where we could learn about one another. While you are making sure that we get things done, I'm making sure that we're doing the right thing, Jenny's making sure that we do it the right way, and Lois is making sure that everybody comes along. I guess it looks like we spend a lot of meeting time on team building, especially for someone who hates meetings. I could drop all of that stuff, but then I don't think we could accomplish our goal of building community. We have to know each other."

Daryl didn't necessarily agree, but he did apologize for his rudeness. We shook hands, walked to our cars, and returned to our paying jobs for the afternoon.

DARLENE REFLECTS AND CHANGES

Now that I had a better understanding of what made Daryl tick, I changed the way I interacted with him. I reevaluated my agendas for the board meetings and decided to have a more businesslike structure for some meetings so that decisionmaking could be accomplished more efficiently. I also made a list of nonurgent tasks, so that whenever Daryl got antsy, I could assign him a task to keep him off my back. All the storage closets are beautifully organized now! Finally, whenever I got an email from Daryl that I thought was too demanding or brusque, I had my husband draft the reply, and I just signed my name to it. My husband could more easily focus on the facts and keep the feelings out of it.

Daryl and I will never be friends, but by figuring out his motivations, I was able to keep him engaged and stay focused on our mission.

Chapter 6 Discussion Questions

What?

1. Describe the context of this case and the leadership choices that you notice throughout the scenario.

So What?

2. What leadership strategies work well for Darlene? What needs work?
3. What facilitation strategies work well for Darlene? What needs work?
4. Are facilitation and leadership ever at odds?
5. How does being a volunteer organization affect how people work with one another?

Now What?

6. What is your most comfortable work style when you work with groups?
7. How do you work with people who are very different from you?

Navigating Conflict

> **Key Topics:** role of consultant, facilitative leadership, Chalk Talk, Continuum Conversations, power relationships, stages of team development
>
> **Key Challenges:** navigating through conflict, surfacing assumptions about power

CONTEXT

Juling is an experienced group facilitator who leads learning communities at her school and across the region. For several years, she has contracted with a local education foundation during the summer to train cohorts of teachers and principals in facilitative leadership, and she organizes Saturday workshops throughout the school year to support these newly trained facilitative leaders.

For the first time, a school district has contacted Juling directly and invited her to develop a weeklong experience for a dozen subject-area curriculum directors to help them function as a learning community and learn strategies for making their work teams more collaborative.

The goal of improved collaboration is severely tested when the supervisor sabotages the agenda by refusing to participate in a discussion. How can educators successfully navigate through conflict, especially if it involves a supervisor or client?

JULING SPEAKS ABOUT HER EXPERIENCE

I felt so flattered to be invited by the Sweet River School District to facilitate a 4-day seminar for the top administrators in their curriculum department.

My good friend Pete had recently started working there and had recommended this training to his direct supervisor, Candace, the associate superintendent of curriculum.

The previous seminars that I had facilitated had been contracted through a local education foundation, so this was the first time I had worked directly with a client to customize a seminar. Candace and I met face-to-face twice during the contracting phase to talk about what supplies would be needed, the terms of payment, and what she hoped the seminar would accomplish. She had a plan, called "Project Unity," for totally reorganizing the curriculum department in ways that she hoped would support collaboration across subject areas and grade levels. Because Pete had assured Candace that facilitative leadership training would introduce everyone in the department to the skills needed for increased collaboration, Candace appointed him to work with me to customize the activities.

Pete was also an experienced facilitator. He had been through a similar training several years earlier and wanted to experience it again with his new colleagues. He was also adamant that he wanted to be a participant rather than a cofacilitator. His fellow participants included the directors of elementary and secondary math, science, social studies, and language arts as well as leaders from fine arts, physical education, and special education. Candace agreed to fully participate as well.

I was eager to work with this group because these participants were already an authentic group that worked together daily throughout the year. Unlike the participants in the summer seminars that I usually led, who came from many different schools and dispersed afterward, these participants could support one another throughout the year as they applied the principles of facilitative leadership to their work. Also, because they had district-level positions, they had the authority to make substantive changes in the district culture and support transformation districtwide.

Pete and I customized the training seminar to take advantage of these opportunities. We tweaked the norm-building process to address long-term collaboration instead of just meeting behaviors. We chose icebreakers and team builders that really delved into personality traits and work styles. Because I knew that newcomers to facilitative leadership are usually euphoric about the training while they are in the middle of it, but often experience discouragement and obstacles after they have returned to their own work settings, Pete and I included several texts about team development in the resource binder.

OFF TO A GOOD START

As expected, the first day of the seminar was busy and productive because the participants were eager to learn new tools for effective collaboration. I laid the foundation by starting with an icebreaker where they chose an artsy postcard to best represent their personal philosophy of education and moved right into an activity in which they wrote about their best ever group experiences and used that to springboard into a norm-construction activity. We talked about the Zones of Comfort, Risk, and Danger (School Reform Initiative, 2014) and agreed that transformative learning takes place in the risky zone. We used a protocol to discuss an article that addressed the transition "From Professional Development to Professional Learning" (Easton, 2008) and engaged in a reflective activity in which participants could discern their personal preferences for working in groups and learn how their colleagues approached group work as well.

The day ended with an incredible Chalk Talk (Smith, cited in School Reform Initiative, 2014) where the team members had a silent conversation around the prompt "What do I want to learn about myself as a curriculum leader?"

The responses addressed wonderings such as [I want to learn . . .]:

- "how to reflect on current practices and improve in order to make a difference for those I lead."
- "how I can use my strengths to grow principals as curriculum leaders on their campuses."
- "how I can keep the work exciting and motivating for me and others who have been doing this for a while."

A few comments led to a flurry of responses with the multicolored markers, and I scrambled to add several feet of butcher paper to the Chalk Talk in order to accommodate the fertile conversation. For example, the comment "I want to know how to use my skills, knowledge, and strengths to support the district's vision in my content area" launched a series of queries such as:

- "What *is* the vision?"
- "Does the district mission gel with my own philosophy and mission?"
- "Who owns the vision? How is it shared?"

The desire "to know how to lead others when change is involved" initiated these reflective responses:

- "I need to know how to change *myself* when I need to."
- "I think this is hard."
- "It is!"
- "Hard but necessary!"

During the debriefing of the Chalk Talk, several participants linked the questions and comments on the butcher paper to specific concerns they had about how Candace's Project Unity was being deployed. Through this discussion, Project Unity emerged as a concrete example of how systemic change, personal change, leadership, and collaboration were linked.

By the end of the day, the group had made great strides in building a respectful working atmosphere and asking questions that got to the heart of their practice as collaborative leaders. The participants' written reflections for the first day indicated that the group appreciated the variety and flow of activities, and one member wrote, "I liked the different ways we could learn the comfort levels or work habits of people in nonthreatening ways." Unfortunately, Candace missed the Chalk Talk and the debriefing session at the end of the day because the head superintendent insisted that she attend a meeting with the superintendent's executive council.

THE CRISIS

Tuesday got off to a horrendous start before I even left my house. Overnight, my partner's car had leaked gasoline all over our garage floor. I was afraid to start my own car's ignition because of the lingering fumes, and our roadside assistance service refused to help until the local fire department came to assess the risk. I didn't have Candace's personal phone number, so I called Pete to let him know that I was running late.

By the time I got to the session, Pete had led the group through the opening moves and icebreaker. Still flustered, I apologized for arriving late and immediately kicked off a series of Continuum Dialogues (Wentworth, cited in School Reform Initiative, 2014) in which the participants respond to prompts by physically placing themselves on an arc and seeing where they stand in relation to others in their group.

So the participants could practice lining up on the arc, I launched the activity with a couple of straightforward questions such as, "How long have you worked for Sweet River School District?" and, "How long have you worked in your current role?" Even these simple prompts provided a venue for the group members to notice that there was a wide range of educational experience and a majority of the team had taken on their current roles within the past 2 years.

Because the group quickly learned how to move along the continuum, I moved to a list of questions that depended more on opinion than fact. I had thought this would be a dynamic way both to delve into some group characteristics and follow up on some of the thought-provoking responses to the Chalk Talk from the previous day when some questions about Project Unity were voiced. Some of the prompts included, "I can clearly articulate the curriculum department's vision," "I believe that collaboration means that everyone must agree," and "I understand how decisions are made in the curriculum department."

Even in my distracted state of mind, I noticed that the participants were hesitating before placing themselves on the arc. There was no laughter or nudging colleagues into place. With arms crossed, Candace stood off to the side and scowled. These questions that addressed how this particular department worked together were sending some participants straight to the danger zone.

Although I recognized the discomfort in the group and realized that Candace probably felt as though her leadership was being attacked, I was at a loss for how to salvage the activity. I stared down at the page where I had scribbled the prompts, but the phrases which last night had seemed like an ingenious way to open up a conversation about leadership, shared vision, and transparency, now just felt mean.

If the participants were ever going to transform into true collaborators, they needed to have a conversation about the power relationships on their team, but their boss was clearly in distress and shutting down.

I rushed through the debriefing, inserted a short break, and went ahead with a text-based discussion that addressed the distinction between facilitation and training. Most of the group members shared a favorite quote and attempted to make a connection with their practice, but with Candace still sulking in silence, the discussion soon fizzled.

The momentum picked up in the afternoon when the participants chose their own groups and practiced using the Consultancy protocol (Dunne, Evans, & Thompson-Grove, cited in School Reform Initiative, 2014) to learn from their dilemmas. Still, I was eager to leave at the end of the day. After collecting the written reflections, I rushed out the door, helped my partner retrieve her car from the repair shop, and picked dinner up at a drive-through. After such a draining day, I felt like a failure and didn't want to interact with anyone at all.

REFLECTING AND REFRAMING

After dinner, I immersed myself in the group's reflections and tried to understand why the day had gone so completely wrong. Several members pointed out the disjointed pacing, and some commented about the change in tone.

One member wrote, "It felt like we moved from an open door to one being slammed shut. I wonder if our group will address the issues of trust or if we will continue as we are." Another requested additional opportunities to address the simmering issues. Reading the participants' reflections gave me hope that there was a critical mass who would courageously engage in hard conversations the next day.

Then I pulled out a journal and a pen and wrote about my own experience for over an hour. I filled several pages with my frustration and questions. I realized that my own physical and mental capacities had been compromised by our car trouble, and that made me less aware and less responsive when the crisis emerged. I saw that the norms we constructed on Monday did not adequately address meeting behaviors. Because the group had not explicitly discussed and recorded a shared understanding of what thoughtful participation looked like, I couldn't just gently refer to the norms when the group was floundering in silence. I was appalled by how leading the prompts for the Continuum Dialogue were. I should have crafted better questions that clearly did not have right or wrong answers. Mostly, I saw how Candace's short absence on the first day had reverberated throughout the next. During the Chalk Talk, the department had teased out concerns about how Project Unity was being rolled out. Their questions about "who owns the vision" were getting at the underlying tension of using top-down methods to reorganize the department in the name of increased collaboration. When I picked up this strand of conversation on Tuesday, Candace felt blindsided. Although I was still frustrated and a little angered by how she had cast a pall on the whole day, I now also sympathized with how disorienting and hurtful the Continuum Dialogue had been for her. I resolved to talk one-on-one with Candace as soon as I could the next morning.

HEALING THE WOUNDS

I arrived so early on Wednesday that the building was still locked. Pete arrived next, opened up the meeting space, and confided that he had gotten little sleep the night before. While I was writing the revamped agenda on poster paper, Candace appeared carrying a huge box of breakfast tacos to share with the group, and before I could approach her, she joined me at the easel and requested a private conversation. We stepped into a nearby conference room, and she admonished me for misrepresenting what the seminar would entail.

She declared, "I thought that you would be teaching us strategies for collaboration. That stuff you did yesterday just split us apart."

"I see that now," I said, nodding.

"Plus, if I want to be quiet, that's my business. You don't know everything that's going on."

"That's true. I don't know everything. Is there anything I need to know about you or the group before we go on?"

She declined, so I showed her the previous day's reflections and remarked that, as an outside facilitator, I thought it was crucial for the group to see her participate. "Candace," I exhorted, "you are the leader. They are looking to you for cues. This group will never truly collaborate unless you model what it means to stay engaged—what it sounds like to listen even when you don't like what you are hearing."

I apologized for my miscues from the day before, acknowledged her vulnerability, and showed her the agenda so she would know what to expect throughout the day. Neither one of us was smiling when we left the room, but we were both determined to do a better job.

MOVING FORWARD

The participant who had volunteered to lead the opening icebreaker had wisely prepared an activity called "Pass the Praise." In our journals, we jotted down every group member's name and then wrote appreciative comments next to each person's name using prompts such as "I respect that...," "You make me laugh when...," and "You have a skill in...." We each then picked one person to publicly praise until everyone in the group had given and received at least one compliment.

That simple activity laid a foundation of professional kindness and appreciation that sustained the group throughout the morning while they studied the article "Stages of Team Development" by Nancy Mohr and Alan Dichter (2002). This short article explicitly describes how collaborative teams may start in a "honeymoon stage" but also go through what they call the "conflict stage," the "confusion-about-democracy stage," the "messy stage," and the "scary stage" before approaching the "mature-group stage."

The 12 group members split into six pairs, and each pair read about one of the stages and prepared a short presentation about that stage of team development. Importantly, I demanded that each pair teach their section to the larger group in an engaging way—no talking heads that just summarized the authors' words.

Through dramatic reenactments, Continuum Dialogues, role-plays, colorful poster presentations, and interactive writing activities, the group members processed the article's main points about leadership and conflict.

Read this article!

Presentation

Several pairs also referred to Project Unity and the uncomfortable tension from the previous day. By drawing on their best teaching selves, the group created a <u>shared understanding of the challenges and prospects of being a collaborative team</u>.

By the end of the day, one member reflected, "We moved toward understanding by working through the processes with authentic work." Another remarked, "It was nice to see how a group can go from tension and conflict to higher functioning!" Having an explicit conversation about the normal conflicts involved in collaborative work allowed this group to learn from the conflict and move forward.

Now, I understand that a facilitator has to bring much more than an agenda and a smile to seminars. I am learning to explain how disruptive true facilitative leadership training can be when I contract with new clients, and I try to embrace conflict as a source of growth and deep learning.

Chapter 7 Discussion Questions

What?

1. List the skills and facilitative strategies that Juling used throughout this scenario.

So What?

2. Which strategies worked? Which were ineffective?
3. What are some other options that Juling could have considered?

Now What?

4. Read the article "Stages of Team Development." List the teams of which you are a member (i.e., department, professional learning community, safety committee, and so on). What stage of development do you think each one is in?
5. Do you have ongoing conflict with anybody at work? How do you manage it?

PART III

Exploring Tensions

The three cases in Part III dig into stubborn dilemmas that permeate the education landscape. These stories move beyond mere knowledge and skill and delve into the negotiations required to learn to work together in communities that help us be our best selves. Chapter 8, "Reclaiming Professional Identity," features a middle school science department that builds a shared vision and goals for improving instruction for English language learners even though external policies and demands are pulling them in a different direction. In Chapter 9, "Honoring Time to Meet and Incorporating Technology," a facilitator struggles with both how to negotiate meeting times that are fair for all and how to incorporate technology while still maintaining confidentiality. Chapter 10, "Developing Cultural Competence," is the personal reflection of a White teacher who seeks ways to overcome her sheltered upbringing and be the kind of knowledgeable, caring, and fierce teacher that her multicultural students and colleagues need her to be.

Reclaiming Professional Identity

Key Topics: teacher evaluation, collegiality, teacher research, professionalism, English language learners, motivation

Key Challenges: maintaining collaboration when competition-inducing policies are implemented

CONTEXT

A highly respected teacher with 20 years of classroom experience, Reginald has led the science department at Willowbend Middle School for over a decade. Hardworking and focused, he has built up a 10-member department with a reputation for collegiality and an engaging curriculum that focuses on real-world science applications. Reginald looks forward to department meetings as a time to interact with friends, discuss current articles about science instruction, and come to consensus about issues that affect all the teachers, such as sharing laboratory resources.

The faculty experiences a crisis in confidence when the school board institutes a teacher bonus system that relies heavily on students' standardized test scores and the local newspaper publishes the teachers' salaries and bonuses on its website. Bitterness threatens to supersede collaboration.

By refocusing on student learning, can this department transform itself into a true community of learners?

REGINALD SPEAKS ABOUT HIS EXPERIENCE

When the bell rang at the end of the day one Wednesday last January, I hurried my 8th-grade science students out the door, grabbed a manila folder, and walked a few doors down the hall to Sharon's classroom for our monthly science department meeting. Along with a few teachers and some brave parents, I had been off campus most of the day with our 8th-graders for our annual field trip to the science museum and planetarium. The buses had returned to school just in time for the afternoon dismissal. No matter how instructive and engaging they might be, field trips are always a bit tiring, so I was looking forward to relaxing with my friends in the science department while we discussed a short article from *Science Scope* and finalized the supply order for the spring semester labs.

Before entering Sharon's room, I stopped off in the supply closet between our classrooms to get a fresh mug of coffee from the pot that Sharon blessedly keeps brewing all day. I also hoped that Margie had remembered to bring her famous pound cake. After chasing kids through the museum and nearby park for the past 4 hours, I needed some caffeine and a snack.

When I sat down at one of the sturdy black lab tables that had been shoved together for our meeting, something seemed off. Jill, a 7th-grade teacher, had a big smirk on her face. Sharon and Margie, best friends who also taught 7th grade, were whispering on the other side of the table and looked up guiltily when I clanked down my mug and prepared to pass out the handouts. The 6th-grade team filed in quietly and sat together on my right. Only Kevin and Phuong, who had been at the museum with the kids and me, were their usual cheerful selves.

THE STORM

"What's up, Margie?" I asked. "You look like you've had a rough day. Did the kids give you a hard time?"

"You know that the kids never bother me. It's always adults that seem to make the most trouble," she countered, and then added, "Haven't you heard? Our teacher bonuses were finally announced today. Not only that, the *Sentinel* posted the bonuses on their website. Everybody can see—parents, kids, coworkers. It's humiliating."

I was surprised at Margie's word choice. Why would such a capable colleague feel humiliated? Still, I was overwhelmingly curious. How did I stack up against the other teachers? I wanted to rush over to the bank of computers on the back wall of the classroom to check out my scores, but I took a deep breath and started to pass out the agenda.

Margie softly interrupted, "Go ahead and look, Reginald. We all know what you're getting in your next paycheck. You should know, too."

She got up and handed me her tablet with the newspaper database up and running. I quickly typed "science teacher" and "Willowbend" into the search boxes to get the scores for our entire department and almost dropped the tablet when I saw that my bonus was the lowest in the department. Phuong grabbed the tablet and then passed it on to Kevin. Their expressions dulled, and Kevin slid the tablet over the table back to me.

I felt angry and embarrassed. What did that number mean?

"Hey, don't take it personally, Reginald," soothed Margie. "We know you're an excellent teacher." She passed me a slice of cake on a paper towel, but I had lost my appetite.

Sharon added, "I'm sure you have something planned for this meeting, but maybe that could wait until next week. I kind of need to process this with you guys. Maybe you can help me make sense of it."

"What's there to make sense of?" crowed Jill. "The most effective teachers get the biggest bonuses. What's wrong with that?"

A quick glance down at the screen confirmed that Jill was getting almost $10,000—the largest bonus available. Margie and Sharon, the other 7th-grade teachers, also had large windfalls.

"Congratulations, Jill," I forced out of my mouth. "I'm happy for you. It's just that I thought our whole department was really effective. I mean, just look at all the amazing labs we do. We're so hands-on. And over 95% of my students passed the state science exam last year. How could I possibly do more?"

"Don't forget all those top-notch field trips you've planned," interjected Kevin.

"The parents love the Star Party you host every year."

"Wasn't it two of your former students who won the state science fair last year and went on to nationals?"

I appreciated their kind words, but then Jill countered, "You know, our department always focuses on teaching style, but the district wants results. It doesn't matter how fancy your lesson plan is if the kids aren't actually learning."

Sharon curtly said, "What if the tests aren't measuring what the students actually need to know?"

"Yeah, blame the test," Jill said. "That's the first attack of teachers who don't want to change."

"Jill! I resent that!" Margie responded. "You know as well as I do that the tests are a problem. We're training our students to ask good questions, be observant, work on teams, persevere. That can't be measured on a bubble test."

"Hey," I cut in. "What I want to know is how the district came up with this number. If our students are scoring well, shouldn't the bonuses reflect that?"

"I read in the union newsletter that it has something to do with improvement," offered Kevin. "They see how much a child has improved from one year to the next. But it's a secret formula. The consultants that came up with the formula say it's proprietary and won't release it."

"How can they possibly tell improvement from year to year?" moaned Trisha, one of the 6th-grade science teachers. "The students take a criterion-based science test in 5th and 8th grade, but our 6th- and 7th-graders take a national norm-referenced test that's not even lined up with our curriculum. Sixth-grade teachers don't stand a chance."

"And it would be hard for an 8th-grade teacher to show his kids made improvements after they had a stellar teacher like me in 7th grade," Jill jabbed.

"What about the subgroups?" I wondered out loud.

Phuong looked daggers at me. "Really, Reginald, I hate it when you use that term. It sounds too much like *subhuman*."

"None of us likes to be reduced to a label or a number," murmured Margie. "That's what I find humiliating, even though I guess I'm supposed to feel gratified by the recognition. This number, that nobody can explain how they calculated, is published far and wide, but the so-called reformers don't even bother to find out what's really going on in our classrooms." She summed it up, "The worst thing is that they've devised a system that tears us apart instead of helping us work together."

[handwritten margin note: Margie]

FEELING DISCONNECTED

While I was driving home that evening, I thought about how my philosophy of teaching didn't fit in with the district's anymore. Maybe these monetary bonuses were designed to inspire us to work harder, but quite frankly, if money were my primary motivation, I would have kept my engineering job in the private sector. Teaching is my third career—after a stint in the military and a couple of years as a civil engineer—and until recently, I had no regrets about making the switch to the classroom 20 years ago. I am a problem-solver, and I thrive on figuring out the best way to teach each science objective. Former students often contact me to let me know that they still remember a particular lab or our extensive fieldtrips where we explored the geology of the state firsthand.

What made me angriest about the bonus system was that it was touted as "objective" and "scientific" in the news article that accompanied the website, but sometimes numbers obscure the truth rather than revealing it. The fact that the magic formula that calculated our bonus was "proprietary" especially stank. How could they possibly make claims about validity when we couldn't even check their arithmetic?

Yet, something that Jill had said still stung because it contained a kernel of truth. Maybe I cared more about my "fancy lesson plans" than about reaching every kid. I might brag about our hands-on lessons, but I knew I wasn't always reaching everybody—especially our small, but growing, population of English language learners.

THE CATALYST

Later that week, Sharon shared an email that she had received from a local education foundation.

"Hey, Reginald, look at this," she squealed. "Here's a chance to get $10,000 for the science department!"

Visions of new equipment filled my head until she went on. "It's a teacher research grant. We can get money to research a question about our practice. The foundation wants to 'enable educators to deepen their work, conduct research inquiries about their practice, and make their work public.'"

"What does that mean?"

"Well, I've been thinking about our meeting earlier this week when we felt so helpless and disrespected by the bonus system. Jill was laughing, but she's upset, too. Honestly, she has no idea why she got a bigger bonus than the rest of us, so how can she possibly replicate it? We need something that will bring us together. We need something that will make us proud to be teachers again."

During our lunch break, Sharon, Margie, and I sat at a table off to the side in the teachers' lounge and looked over the request for proposals. We had just a couple of weeks to put the plan together, but it looked doable. I ran our idea past our principal before we proceeded and then called a special meeting to see if the science department could build a consensus around a research question and quickly prepare a timeline and budget.

When we met after school, it didn't take long to agree on a topic to explore. One good thing that had come from the state accountability system was that it did shine a light on how Willowbend's test scores might be good overall, but the English language learners' scores were far behind. Meeting their needs was an ongoing challenge.

We were used to having Spanish-speaking and Vietnamese-speaking families in our community, but recently we were also enrolling children who spoke Kiswahili, Kinyarwanda, Nepali, and other languages. Our principal insisted on enrolling the English language learners in regular content classes instead of sheltered classes ever since he heard about a Vietnamese girl at another school who learned Spanish before she learned English because the ESL kids spent all day together instead of interacting with native English speakers.

Although Jill joked that it wouldn't be in her best interests financially to assist us since her future bonuses might be jeopardized if all the school's students improved in comparison with hers, the department agreed that learning how to better teach English language learners would make the biggest impact on our school. Our focusing question for this teacher-as-researcher project was: *As a department, how can the science teachers improve the academic achievement of our students who are nonnative speakers of English?*

*research question

RESULTS

It's been a little over a year since that horrible department meeting that started us on this journey. Our proposal was funded, but it's been hard to regain our collegial vibe with so many personnel changes.

After more than 30 years of service, Margie took advantage of an early retirement package and got a part-time position at a private school. She confided that she still loves teaching, but the toxic district policies made her feel like an automaton. Kevin left to attend business school, and Trisha took an entire semester of leave to stay home with her infant.

Still, the very act of writing the grant proposal helped the department members clarify our thinking and focus on our students' needs. We spent a large portion of the grant funds on getting professional development that was directly related to improving the academic achievement of students who are nonnative speakers of English. Phuong hooked us up with a university professor from her master's program who researches language acquisition, and most of us took a multiday inservice that was spread out over the summer and a few days in the fall semester.

I have learned that my hands-on approach was an admirable start, but it wasn't enough to serve the English language learners in my classes. I learned that I needed to do some intense direct instruction around academic English related to science, so now my lab is full of word walls, all students develop personal dictionaries, and the teachers have collaborated with our district's media center to develop more visual aids. We've also become more conscious of our questioning styles and interaction patterns by videotaping or observing one another's classes.

Importantly, the content of our department meetings has changed, too. Instead of just getting together and discussing a random article, we now use the time to look at student work and examine our lesson plans. The newcomers to our faculty have noted that they enjoy being part of a true learning community. We use grant funds to pay for a modest stipend so we can all stay later, and examining the work has helped all of us stay focused on student learning. It also helped us tease out assumptions about our priorities and values. Who are we really working for? The students? Our administrators? Taxpayers?

An added benefit of winning the grant is that the sponsoring foundation hosts support meetings for all the groups in our region that were funded. When the Willowbend science department met with research teams from other schools, we saw how teachers from surrounding districts felt battered by the testing culture, too.

I have also learned that our inquiry has only just begun. We will have to continually look at what we've learned, how it's working and what changes need to be made in order to help the kids. Our midyear assessments have shown a marked improvement for all students, not just the English language learners, so we believe that many of these strategies are having a positive effect.

This research project revealed how I want to make my practice public—not with scores and bonuses published in the newspaper, but by networking with other teachers in a meaningful way. We still teach in a system that is turning teaching and learning into commodities, but taking on the challenge of coming up with our own solutions has helped us reclaim our passion for teaching.

Chapter 8 Discussion Questions

What?

1. Describe the context of this case and the leadership choices that you notice throughout the scenario.

So What?

2. What conditions can the teachers influence? What is beyond their influence?
3. What role do emotions (embarrassment, anger, humiliation, confusion, pride, concern, and so forth) play in this scenario?
4. What role do relationships play in this scenario?

Now What?

5. How do you include inquiry or research in your own professional development?
6. What does it mean to be a "professional"?

Honoring Time to Meet and Incorporating Technology

> *Key Topics:* reflective practice, responding to skepticism, virtual meetings, blogging
>
> *Key Challenges:* negotiating conflicting schedules, establishing an online community, maintaining confidentiality

CONTEXT

An experienced chemistry teacher and teacher leader, Lannitra facilitates an inquiry group of 10 science teachers who are part of a school and university collaborative that was designed to improve K–12 science instruction by both deepening teachers' content knowledge and encouraging reflective practice through teacher inquiry. About 60 teachers meet once a month on Saturday mornings with university faculty who lead engaging demonstration lessons that refresh and improve content knowledge. Lannitra's smaller group meets once a month on a Thursday evening to engage in activities that encourage reflective practice. The program requires a 2-year commitment from the participating teachers, and they earn a small stipend for attending a minimum number of meetings each year.

Lannitra's group does substantial work during its first year together, but it is in danger of disbanding when some participants move away and increasing external demands on the teachers' time impinge on the planned meeting times. When the group experiments with using technology to have online meetings, complications arise concerning confidentiality. What can Lannitra do to keep this group engaged and moving forward with reflective practices?

LANNITRA SPEAKS ABOUT THE PROGRAM

I've really enjoyed being a mentor and facilitating teacher in the Reflective Science Teacher Initiative (RSTI), a professional development program that is cosponsored by a prestigious university and the local public school system. Several dozen K–12 science teachers meet on Saturdays in labs and classrooms at the university where faculty members deepen our content knowledge by demonstrating innovative lessons and labs. It's fun to play the part of a student again, and the discussions after the labs help us build up our pedagogical content knowledge. We talk about common scientific misconceptions that our students have and share strategies for teaching and reteaching a wide range of objectives.

This is invaluable because principals, especially at the Title I schools, have a hard time filling all the science teacher openings. They might have a history major who happened to minor in science fill a vacancy, or somebody with an advanced degree in biology might end up taking on a few sections of chemistry or physics. Because so many science teachers in our system are teaching outside of their fields of study, it's super helpful to get refreshers on all that content knowledge.

Our inquiry group, which meets on one Thursday each month at the high school where I teach, includes 10 teachers who work on the south side of town. Jeff and Diana teach at the high school with me. Kerry, Cindy, Akilah, Aretha, and Brittany are split between the three junior highs. Justin and Jimmy Don are two science lab teachers from elementary schools who were recruited into the program, too.

Our time together on Thursdays focuses less on science content and more on learning tools for reflective practice. *Reflection* is a complicated term that might refer to simply thinking about the past, examining oneself and one's practice, or changing one's practice and one's identity. The theory of action for the project is that if teachers explicitly learn how to examine their own practice critically, then their instruction will continue to improve throughout their careers.

In the program, the demonstration lessons provide "contextual anchors" (Aubusson, Griffin, & Steele, 2010) for teaching reflective practice. The participants keep journals with entries where they respond to the demonstration lessons and make connections to their own work. We also talk about critical incidents that happen in our classrooms, and we use protocols to nurture reflective discourse when we examine student work and bring in teaching dilemmas. All the while, I'm trying to get all the participants to move past simple descriptions of what happened and really analyze their experiences.

VALUING INTERACTION

At our very first Thursday meeting, Justin—one of the elementary science lab teachers—asked if our inquiry group could ever meet online instead of face-to-face.

"Why?" I queried. "Why does meeting online appeal to you, Justin?"

"Mainly so I could get home sooner, let the dog out, and relax a bit before having another 2- or 3-hour work obligation. This meeting place is close to work but far from home."

"Those are important concerns, Justin," I stalled. "I'd prefer to meet face-to-face for the first few months so we can get to know one another and build up some esprit de corps, but I'm open to revisiting your concerns later this year."

Honestly, I don't quite trust the idea of working online for these kinds of collaborative projects. I understand the appeal of balancing work and home obligations and of getting to wear sweatpants to work, but I fear that if we had virtual meetings, the participants would be scrolling through social media or catching up on grading instead of paying attention to one another. Plus, I just don't know how to manage it.

I really appreciate the way the Reflective Science Teacher Initiative brings science teachers together to talk about our craft, and I enjoy seeing colleagues from across our public school system on the Saturdays that we meet at the university. I don't want to jeopardize any of the social aspects of our inquiry group by taking the meetings online.

A GREAT FIRST YEAR

The first year of the Reflective Science Teacher Initiative has been such a pleasure. In addition to the energizing Saturday sessions led by the university, our inquiry group met face-to-face eight times and did substantial work. Each participant was provided with time and space to get personalized feedback about their own questions of practice.

Learning to Question

At first, some group members were skeptical. Jeff, the AP physics teacher on my campus, complained, "This doesn't seem like a real science inservice to me. 'Reflection' sounds like something those poetry-loving English teachers do. How can journaling possibly improve my units about force and motion or electromagnetism?"

Fortunately, the mentor training had prepared me for this scenario. I replied, "Jeff, reflective practice *is* science. Like all scientists, we're asking important questions—and our questions happen to be about our teaching practice. Our teaching experiences, observations, and artifacts are data that we can examine together. Our journals are like lab notebooks that capture our experiences. These monthly meetings are laboratories where we seek evidence of student learning and our own growth. The word *reflection* doesn't just address our personal, subjective feelings. The act of reflection is like the scientific analysis of evidence with the discussion of implications that we'd see in any top-rated research journal. Just because we aren't talking about probability levels and standard deviation doesn't mean that our personal inquiries aren't significant."

By mapping the reflective practices that we were learning onto research concepts that they already respected or revered, I helped the group embrace teacher inquiry. My colleagues eagerly brought their own questions and dilemmas to our shared table. The range of topics embedded in the questions indicated that they wanted to examine a broad range of teaching issues beyond gaining deeper content knowledge. Here are some examples:

- Jimmy Don asked, "How can I make sure that my students get all the lab materials that they deserve without spending hundreds of dollars of my own money?"
- Cindy wondered, "My principal requires a minimum number of grades per marking period. How can I make grading the volume of student work more manageable? Can I give grades for participation in a discussion?"
- Akilah inquired, "This grading rubric didn't work. How can I improve it?"
- Jeff asked, "How do I keep high school seniors motivated during the spring semester?"

Evidence of a Team

The participants also became more reflective throughout the year. In the fall, when I prompted them to reflect about the meeting, they would often just describe what had happened and maybe how they felt about it. By the end of the school year, almost everybody was making connections between what we did together and what happened in their own classrooms.

I was also heartened to see that the participants thought fondly of our inquiry group. At our final meeting in May of the first year, Cindy wrote, "I love how thoughtful and dedicated our group is! Everyone is so great at providing support and their wisdom. Honestly, I was a reluctant participant at our first meeting, but I've changed my tune. I feel like a more thoughtful teacher and person because of this group."

Akilah gushed, "I love this group. I am amazed and impressed at the intellectual curiosity and the passion that everyone brings to the table. Next year I hope we can push ourselves further."

Justin, who started the year with a plea for meeting online, wrote, "I have been to many professional developments, but our science inquiry group has easily been the most meaningful. It was great meeting dedicated teachers with great insight about the class and life."

By the end of our first year together, we had accomplished so much, and I was delighted that we could look forward to another year of learning from one another.

ENCOUNTERING SNAGS

Our inquiry group lost two members over the summer. Both Kerry and Diana had completed their 2-year teaching commitments through an organization that places college graduates in high-needs classrooms. We knew that Kerry planned on leaving the classroom to attend medical school, but Diana departed, too, to take a job with a biomedical research firm. I was sad to see them go. Our inquiry group was now down to eight members.

When I reached out to everyone else in August to confirm our meeting times for the upcoming academic year, Aretha inquired about switching to a different day of the week because she was embarking on a master's degree program and needed to take some night classes. The consensus among the other group members was that it was more convenient to stick with Thursday, so Aretha arranged her class schedule around our group.

Overcoming Distance

We also learned that Jimmy Don had accepted a position as the lead science educator at a beautiful camp in a forested area about a hundred miles from our meeting place. Getting to work in both science and outdoor education was Jimmy Don's dream job, and since he was technically still an employee of the public school system, he was still eligible to participate in the Reflective Science Teacher Initiative. Jimmy Don asked if he could Skype into the weeknight meetings because attending in person would require 4 hours of driving.

With both a kind demeanor and the ability to craft insightful probing questions, Jimmy Don had been a model group member during the first year. I really wanted to keep him in our inquiry group, so I told him we'd work out a way to accommodate him, but I had no idea how that would work.

Negotiating Time

At our first meeting in September, everybody except Jimmy Don was able to meet in my classroom as usual. We all brought our calendars and scheduled our monthly inquiry meetings for the rest of the year. We tried to stick with the third Thursday of the month, but changed it to the second Thursday of October to work around Brittany's school's open house and the fourth Thursday in March to avoid spring break. I contend that whatever event gets on a calendar first should be honored. As other opportunities come up, you should accept or decline according to the commitments that you already have.

Before our second meeting, Brittany—an early-career teacher who taught an innovative combination math and science class at her middle school—contacted me to let me know that her principal insisted that she help staff the after-school math tutorial program, and it conflicted with our science inquiry meetings. Brittany was distraught. Of all the teachers in our group, she benefitted most from the collegiality and support.

I was very angry that Brittany's principal didn't support her work in our inquiry group this year even though he had signed off on her participation the year before. Although working as a math tutor was officially voluntary, Brittany was afraid that the principal would "get back at her" if she declined. Once again, I went to the group to see if we could accommodate Brittany by shifting the start time of our meetings to 90 minutes later. As soon as I sent an email inquiry to the group, Aretha contacted me privately:

> I'm just letting you know I feel it's unfair for the group to keep accommodating one person. We set the dates and made changes because of her open house, now the group has to adjust again? Well, if that be the case, can the group accommodate me as well and change the meeting day to another day of the week instead of Thursdays? I think it's only fair, if we change for one person, we should be able to change for everyone in the group!

Aaaaagh! My values for both preserving a predictable meeting schedule and being flexible enough to keep everybody engaged came in direct conflict.

I made the executive decision to stick with our original schedule, and attendance plummeted throughout the fall semester: Cindy had ongoing car problems, Justin's principal scheduled Family Science Night on one of our meeting dates, and then our town got hit pretty hard by the flu virus. I got headaches whenever one of our meeting dates approached. The purpose of the group was to improve science instruction, and I couldn't even get my group in the same room at the same time. I didn't have the capacity or the power to negotiate with all these principals who insisted that their teachers attend things besides our inquiry meetings. I'm a teacher, too.

TRYING OUT TECHNOLOGY

Conducting meetings with only half of the original participants present left me feeling forlorn. The grant stipulated that each participant had to attend a minimum of eight inquiry meetings a year in order to receive the stipend. If we continued to meet according to our original plan, Brittany would almost certainly have to drop out, but changing the meeting time inconvenienced others. If I did nothing to reschedule, then some group members would lose their stipends. Our situation really brought into relief questions of who got accommodated.

Video Calls

My first step was to ensure that Jimmy Don could stay engaged by attending the meeting through a video call. This was way outside my comfort zone. I feel that I am a skilled facilitator because I have a gift for connecting with people, planning effective meetings, and facilitating protocols when needed. Now I also had to learn how to coordinate technology and troubleshoot technical difficulties.

This hybrid system—with most of us meeting in person and Jimmy Don appearing on a laptop—also added a layer of planning. Any student work that we were sharing had to be scanned and emailed to Jimmy Don so he could participate in the feedback sessions, and I no longer had the freedom to bring in a short article to read and discuss at the last minute if it struck my fancy. Everything had to be planned ahead of time in order to include Jimmy Don. Soon, I quit incorporating activities that required us to get up and move around like Chalk Talk, Affinity Map, and Continuum Dialogue. This new situation definitely put a crimp in my facilitation style.

Blogging

In order to keep participants engaged in our work between meetings, I began experimenting with a blog. It made our practice public and added an interactive component to our reflections. After each meeting, I posted a summary of our activities as well as every member's written reflections. We took privacy precautions such as using pseudonyms, and I avoided posting photos of people, but I did post photos of some of our artifacts like a Chalk Talk that we composed at the beginning of the year. Whenever somebody had to miss a meeting, he or she could read the blog to see what we did, and each member could add comments that expressed his or her own thinking and learning. These comments enlivened the blog by turning the reflections into a conversation instead of a monologue:

> Cindy commented, "This is my first time responding in this medium, and I'm amazed by the different modes of sharing technology provides us. I find great value in having a 'voice,' but more value in being able to share it in this way and get feedback."

> Akilah concurred, "I love the quick posting of everyone's thoughts. It makes my own reflection of the meeting more insightful and deep."

The blog strengthened our inquiry group by providing a way to sustain the conversation of our multicampus group in between meetings and producing an ongoing record of our work together. Most important, maintaining the blog actually helped me reflect on my reflections. Studying the entries over time helped me see connections and reinforce the good work that we do for students and for one another.

THE DARK SIDE OF REMOVING BOUNDARIES

We had found a new normal. With each meeting, I got more comfortable and skilled with including Jimmy Don through the video call. Because the technology was no longer scary, we all agreed to experiment with group video calls for a couple of "makeup" meetings so that everyone could get credit for enough meetings to earn the stipend.

I was also delighted with how the blog helped us stay engaged, and I even liked the public aspect of blogging. It seemed like a great way to both display what the Reflective Science Teacher Initiative was achieving and model how reflective practice was making a difference for local science education. Boy, was I naïve.

The Chalk Talk that I had photographed and posted on the blog was a discussion around the question, "What barriers to reflective practice do you face?" Someone had written "War Room" on the Chalk Talk and had explained that campus leaders had an excruciatingly narrow view of which student products were worthy of discussion. There was such an emphasis on standardized test scores that one assistant principal had turned a conference room into a "war room" where every child's scores were posted and student names on magnetized strips could be shifted around after each benchmark test according to who had mastered each objective.

This thread of conversation was picked up in the blog, and Aretha had commented about how her middle school campus's emphasis on benchmark testing had taken so many days out of her schedule for classroom instruction. There was so much stress on benchmarks that there was no room for rich, reflective discourse. The answers to the critical questions of what we expect our students to learn, how will we know they are learning, and how will we respond when they don't learn (DuFour, DuFour, Eaker, & Karhanek, 2004) had been contorted to, "We expect our students to learn what's on the test, we'll know they are learning when we test them, and if they don't learn, we'll test them some more!"

Unfortunately, Aretha's principal stumbled across our online discussion and was angered and embarrassed by Aretha's honest assessment of what was going on at that middle school. He deduced who was involved and confronted Aretha. At our next face-to-face meeting, Aretha said that she no longer felt safe contributing to the blog and requested that none of us mention her or her school in our posts, even with pseudonyms.

In my attempts to redesign the way the group interacted in order to make it more available, I had unwittingly turned our haven of reflective practice and inquiry into just another setting for teachers to feel beaten down.

Chapter 9 Discussion Questions

What?

1. What challenges does this team face when it comes to negotiating a time to meet?
2. How does Lannitra change her practice in order to accommodate her inquiry group?

So What?

3. What are the purposes of professional reflection?
4. What values guide Lannitra's decisionmaking in this scenario?

Now What?

5. What new skills do you need in order to better serve the groups that you lead?
6. How will you get these skills?

Developing Cultural Competence

Key Topics: equity, dialogue, reflective practice

Key Challenges: surfacing deeply ingrained assumptions, talking about race, taking the time to transform

CONTEXT

Debbie Bell is a White history teacher and department chairperson at a large comprehensive high school that struggles to have equitable outcomes for children regardless of race, ethnicity, language, or socioeconomic status. In an attempt to address the glaring achievement gaps, district administrators mandate that all the mid-level K–12 teacher leaders, such as department chairs and grade-level chairs, attend a 2-day "culture training" workshop in the summer.

During portions of the workshop, Debbie observes a friend who is silenced and disrespected. She feels that the facilitators, a team of consultants who were brought in from another state, assume that Debbie and the other White teachers have nothing to offer in the conversations about race and class. What are the implications for Debbie's work as a facilitative leader on her campus?

DEBBIE SPEAKS ABOUT HER EXPERIENCE

When I found out that the school system was offering cultural training during the summer, I was excited about the opportunity. I live and teach in a community that is becoming more and more diverse every year, and over the course of many years as a social studies teacher, I have sometimes struggled to connect with all of my students.

Honestly, my own upbringing in a predominantly White suburb of a large city was rather sheltered. I was not concerned with race back then because almost all of my classmates looked like me. In my own 13 years of K–12 schooling, I remember having one African American teacher and just a handful of African American classmates. Asian, Latino, and Jewish families provided what little diversity there was, and being colorblind was considered to be polite.

The land grant university that I went to was also rather bland when it came to diversity. My first experiences with multicultural communities came during my first year of teaching in the large, urban school district where I still teach today. I knew I had a lot to learn when I was confronted with an unfair tracking system that put the White and middle-class children of color in the honors track, but my regular class had only one White child in it. It was obviously unfair, and the students in that regular class gave me a trial by fire.

Over the years, I've tried to build bridges across differences, and I've worked hard to dismantle our school's unfair tracking system. Still, I figured that any extra knowledge or skill that I could glean from the culture training would be helpful to me and my students.

THE IMPERATIVE FOR MULTICULTURAL EDUCATION

The workshop took place at a nearby high school where the participants gathered in the auditorium, and I knew that the district had put a lot of resources into this workshop when the superintendent himself greeted us from the podium with a short pep talk about providing better instruction for all our students. Then the director of the research and accountability department gave a really interesting presentation about demographic trends in our region. She made the point that our whole nation is becoming more diverse and educators need to know how to reach all people. Besides pointing out the demographic trends, she also shared research that showed that measures of social capital and civic engagement are negatively correlated with ethnic diversity (Putnam, 2007), so it is imperative that we proactively build trust and build a sense of community in our classrooms.

So far, this was sounding right up my alley. I already valued nurturing a sense of community in my classes. I just wanted to learn more strategies for helping it happen. The final speaker in the auditorium was the lead facilitator from the team of consultants. She gave a rousing speech about the transformative nature of multicultural education and concluded with a quote from James Banks (2007):

> An important goal of multicultural education is to improve race relations and to
> help all students acquire the knowledge, attitudes, and skills needed to participate

in cross-cultural interactions and in personal, social, and civic action that will help make our nation more democratic and just. Multicultural education is consequently as important for middle-class White suburban students as it is for students of color who live in the inner city. Multicultural education fosters the public good and the overarching goals of the commonwealth. (p. viii)

With that inspiration about justice and democracy ringing in our ears, the teachers filed out of the auditorium and found our assigned classrooms for the seminars.

DISAPPOINTMENT AND DISILLUSIONMENT

When I got to my assigned classroom, I eased myself into one of the student desks and looked around. My good friend and colleague Jack was in the room, too. We noticed that there were already some norms posted on the whiteboard. They were:

Show up (or choose to be present),
Pay attention (to heart and meaning),
Tell the truth (without blame or judgment), and
Be open to outcome (not attached to outcome).

I liked the fact that these norms addressed the need to be open and truthful while we learned about building multicultural communities. However, as an experienced meeting facilitator myself, I wondered if there needed to be some more specific guidelines for meeting behaviors. What does "showing up" look like? Is it merely being in the room? Does it include being on time and listening attentively? Teachers can be the toughest audience imaginable, so I wondered how that would play out in our fairly large group of 30 participants.

When it was time to get started, our consultant introduced herself and we quickly introduced ourselves with just our names, schools, and subjects taught. I knew some of the other social studies teachers, but most of the people in the room were either strangers or people I just recognized by sight.

On that first day, we heard a mini-lecture about focusing on student learning, broke for lunch, and reconvened in the auditorium to watch a short film about challenging cultural stereotypes. The presentations on that first day were interesting but in no way transformative. I felt a pinprick of discomfort during the film when I recognized some of the stereotypes that I sometimes lazily accepted, but overall I felt like we barely scratched the surface. I realized that the norms did not need to address meeting behaviors because the participants were not expected to interact much, anyway.

On the second day, we went immediately to our classrooms, and our facilitator divided us into smaller groups for a text-based discussion about a short article that had been assigned as homework. It addressed exploring racial identity and cultivating trust. We used a protocol called Three Levels of Text (Southern Maine Partnership, cited in School Reform Initiative, 2014) whereby we each read aloud a passage we had selected, said what we thought about the passage, and then said what we thought the implications for our work were. Then our small group responded to what the speaker said. I thought it was a great way for everybody to have a say and listen to one another. I was also blessed to have two African American teachers in my group who brought up points that I had not thought about. This was exactly what I had hoped to encounter at this workshop.

During the time set aside for debriefing, the classroom got really loud. I caught my friend Jack's eye from across the room and wondered why he looked so still and quiet. I found Jack during the lunch break. As we sat down with our box lunches, I asked, "What's wrong, Jack? I could hear your group having a spirited conversation from across the room, but you seemed kind of quiet."

"Debbie, that group was not having a conversation. I thought that the article was thought provoking, but when I tried to add something to the conversation, the group leader looked right at me and said, 'We don't need to hear the voice of a White man.' I thought, 'Okay, you won't be hearing anything from me the rest of the day.'"

"Are you serious?! Weren't you using the protocol? Our small group used the Three Levels of Text. We all got to talk and we all listened in timed rounds."

"Well, we started off using it, but this consultant must really have a chip on her shoulder. She's White, but I get the feeling that she wants to prove that she is more advanced and enlightened than us White folks down here."

"What are you going to do this afternoon? We're supposed to spend more time in our small groups after lunch for the conversations about disrupting inequality."

"I guess I'll go back since I promised to 'Be Present.' But I resent being shut down like that. Believe me, I have a more nuanced view of privilege than that consultant can imagine. I totally understand the fact that people that look like me have been too loud and too arrogant and too unfair for too long. But I'm afraid that I'm going to have to tell that consultant that I'm gay for her to listen to me."

Jack really was gay, but he tended to have a "Don't ask; don't tell" attitude at work. I wondered if Jack's facilitator thought that she was doing us a service by pushing us to a deeper understanding of privilege. I was put off by the "holier than thou" attitude that ended up squelching learning instead of encouraging dialogue.

DEBBIE'S PERSONAL HISTORY

My own sense of not being particularly privileged was wrapped in my working-class roots. Our home was always full of books, but neither of my parents went to college. Dad started working full-time at a factory when he was barely a teenager.

Soon after my parents married they moved to a newly built suburban subdivision filled with small brick homes. After little more than a decade, larger and more-expensive houses surrounded our modest neighborhood. My two sisters and I went to junior high and high school with classmates whose parents were upper-middle-class professionals. Some were even quite wealthy. Even though the three of us were high academic achievers and had friends from all walks of life, I often felt underprivileged. For example, I have a vivid memory of riding on a school bus filled with band members on our way to a marching band contest. As the bus was driving past the outskirts of my neighborhood, one of the tuba players derisively pointed to the houses, which admittedly looked a little shabby, and said, "My dad says that all those houses should be bulldozed, and they should build bigger houses for better people to move in."

I was indignant that the boy and his father equated being a "better person" with being wealthy. I also was completely silent—too embarrassed and unsure of myself to confront the tuba player and speak the truth: the truth that the run-down neighborhood was filled with kind, hardworking people and the truth that my dad was probably smarter and evidently nicer than the tuba player's father, but Dad's chances for finding meaningful, higher-paying work were limited by growing up in poverty and not finishing school. That incident on the bus made me feel angry, isolated, and silenced—like Jack felt today.

DEVELOPING PEARLS OF WISDOM

After the workshop, I kept thinking about how the assumptions that people have about one another get in the way of true understanding. I know that I have a long way to go, but I've also had some important experiences over the past few years that have helped me think about race. These educative experiences often began with an irritation or frustration. Like an oyster that covers an irritant with layers of nacre to form a luminescent pearl, I realized that these irritations and the resulting reflections were reforming my practices and transforming my identity. I hoped to someday have created my own metaphorical string of pearls of wisdom and understanding.

Layer One—Racial Awareness

My musings took me back to my first year of teaching at a nearby middle school. With so few multiracial experiences under my belt and with almost no previous reflection about my own cultural identity, I was unprepared to teach in a multiethnic school when I began my career right after college. In my hometown, race was invisible. In diverse schools, it is not. During that first year of teaching 7th-grade history, I had a very challenging student in my second-period "regular" class. Alton was usually tardy, always loud, didn't do classwork or homework, and even actively disrupted the class by throwing wads of paper and walking around the room during instruction. After listening to my daily reports of Alton's disruptive conduct for 2 weeks, my teammates advised me that I needed to call his parents before I could send Alton to the assistant principal.

I finally got up the courage and dialed his number. A boy, most likely Alton himself, answered. Using the telephone manners my White mother had taught me, I said, "Hello. May I please speak with Mrs. Jefferson?" Without saying a word to me, the boy yelled, "Mama! Some White woman wants to talk to you!"

That was my first personal experience with understanding that White was more than a skin color because the boy had pegged me as "White" just by the sound of my voice. Furthermore, from his tone, I could infer that a White woman calling his home was an unusual experience and that he was not happy about it.

I was irritated, but that irritation led to awareness of my own Whiteness.

Layer Two—Building Understanding

Fortunately for me and my development as a teacher, I had been assigned to a very supportive team who easily modeled respecting multiple viewpoints because we were so diverse ourselves. Violet, the language arts teacher, was an elegant African American lady with over 20 years of teaching experience. Ruth, a middle-aged Jewish woman with a sharp sense of humor, demanded participation from every student when she taught math, while Ruby, the science teacher, was an energetic, African American, single mother whose sparkling smile often softened her tough demeanor. I rounded out the team as the eager Anglo girl fresh out of college to teach social studies. I wondered if I would ever be able to successfully teach the most demanding students who were so different from me, but the fact that I saw these same students be successful and engaged in Violet's, Ruth's, and Ruby's classrooms next door and across the hall gave me hope that someday I could reach the students, too. Importantly, seeing the students become successful in my teammates' classes made it painfully obvious that their lack of achievement in my class was not all their fault. It was mine.

My teaching team talked candidly about race. This was a new experience for me. I was also taken aback when some of my students asked me questions about race as well. Sometimes with humor and sometimes with frustration, my students pushed me to see them with new eyes. For example, LaKeisha, a girl in my homeroom, looked curiously at me one morning and asked, "Miss Bell, why do White people come to school with wet hair all the time? Y'all look like a bunch of wet rats." I laughed and the whole class got into a discussion about our different hair care routines.

Less funny was the time that several Black girls in second period demanded, "Miss Bell, how come whenever you talk about Black people, all you ever talk about is slavery?" The answer seemed simple to me. It was a Texas history course, and we had not yet gotten to the year 1865 and emancipation. However, their courageous question made me realize how difficult it would be to sit in class after class without ever seeing a positive image of the group I identified with. In response, the following year, Violet and I worked together and started the year off with a shared research assignment about 20th- and 21st-century Texans. Every student could choose his or her own topic, but we made sure that the list was full of admirable politicians, community organizers, businesspeople, musicians, and athletes who represented all ethnicities. The irritation of being accused of systemic racism in my classroom led to an important change in practice that made my classroom more welcoming for all.

Layer Three—Cultural Conversations

As I reflected about my own experiences, I realized how ridiculous it was to think that a 2-day summer workshop could really help us transform into adept teachers in multicultural contexts. I realized that we needed ongoing conversation that would challenge us.

Jack and I talked to our principal about a program we had heard about from friends at another school. Called "Cultural Conversations," the program involved bringing volunteer teachers from different ethnic groups together once a week to talk about our own experiences, discuss important literature related to multicultural teaching, and actually apply what we were learning to our own campus.

Because the program took place over several weeks, instead of being crammed into just a couple of days, there was time to reflect. Most important, we had heard that the facilitator was a lovely person who would take us to a better place by holding our hands and pulling us along instead of pushing us over.

UNCOVERING ASSUMPTIONS

It was during a Cultural Conversations meeting that I had my first experience with Peggy McIntosh's (1989) article "White Privilege: Unpacking the Invisible Knapsack." Ten teachers, half of us Black and half White, had committed to gathering weekly in our school's professional library to learn more about one another and how to better serve all our racially diverse students.

In one of the early sessions, we took some time to complete and discuss McIntosh's survey. I felt shock and disbelief when I saw the large discrepancy in scores between my Black and White colleagues. These talented, respected, and amazingly effective Black teachers like Violet and Ruby navigated through life under the strain of burdens that I could barely imagine. The survey revealed truths about how different our daily experiences were even though we lived in the same city and taught in the same school.

It was a transformative moment—for the first time in my life, I truly felt privileged to be White, and I almost threw up.

As we moved through the course, we also had opportunities to read and discuss alternative history texts. I realized that part of what makes building multicultural communities so difficult is that it forces all of us, and especially those of us in the dominant culture, to face the painful contradictions of our culture. Patricia Ramsey (2004) reminds us that "by accepting and codifying these contradictions [of stealing land from Indians and enslaving Africans], our forefathers established the precedent that private ownership, material wealth, and profits take precedence over the ideals of liberty and equality" (p. 5). The contradictions affect the curriculum and teacher-student relationships at all levels of schooling.

TAKING ACTION AS A FACILITATOR

Uncovering assumptions is one of the basic roles of a facilitator, so uncovering big assumptions about race, ethnicity, and privilege is huge. If we are ignoring these big assumptions, how can we possibly work on the smaller things? Also, my experiences at the workshop made me understand how important a facilitator is in creating an atmosphere in which sharing and transformation can take place.

I've seen advertisements that claim that pearls are a unique jewel because they have a "soft inner glow." I aspire to have a soft inner glow of understanding as I facilitate and lead others.

Chapter 10 Discussion Questions

What?

1. Describe the events of the culture training workshop.
2. Describe Jack's experience at the workshop.

So What?

3. How does Debbie's background affect her sense of self?
4. Does this case sound truthful? Does anything surprise you about Debbie's experiences?

Now What?

5. What are the irritants in your professional or personal life that have helped you see the world in a different way?
6. How have you reacted to the irritants?
7. Does reflective practice help you form new "pearls" of better understanding and wisdom?

PART IV

Tying It All Together

The final chapter takes a close look at the role of the facilitator in leading collaborative and reflective learning and analyzes what effective facilitators know, what they do, and who they are.

Conclusion: Reflecting on the Role of the Facilitator

Key Topics: facilitation knowledge, facilitation skills, facilitator traits

Key Challenges: developing skilled facilitators, identifying skilled facilitators

---

CONTEXT

Jacob works at a nonprofit organization whose mission includes improving student outcomes in public schools by developing teacher leaders and reducing turnover in the teaching profession. The organization is planning a regional education summit that will take place over 3 days in July. Around 300 teachers, principals, professors, policymakers, and other community members are expected to gather at a large hotel to think deeply about student engagement. Besides hearing keynote addresses from national speakers and attending planned workshops where they can learn about local best practices, the 300 participants will also be assigned to a "home group" of about 20 participants who will meet for part of each day. The purpose of these home groups is to create a space that encourages deeper dialogue and sharing among educators who might not normally interact.

The planning committee at the nonprofit has tasked Jacob to be in charge of both creating a flexible agenda for the home group portion of the institute and recruiting 30 experienced facilitators to cofacilitate the home groups. What should Jacob keep in mind as he seeks out skillful facilitators to lead the home groups at the institute?

JACOB SPEAKS ABOUT HIS EXPERIENCE

The organization that I work for has long been an advocate for reflective practice and facilitative leadership in local schools. I first became connected with their programs when I was a classroom teacher, and I joined their staff 2 years ago to work on several initiatives related to developing teacher leaders.

Each summer, I help train several cohorts of educators to be facilitative leaders. The curriculum for the facilitative leadership training might change a bit from session to session in order to meet the needs of the participants, but there are always experiences related to developing norms, giving and receiving feedback, valuing different voices, and using a variety of protocols. I also schedule monthly workshops on Saturdays to help support the newly trained facilitators with topics such as creating meaningful agendas, developing a portfolio, choosing protocols, and using team builders. Over the years, our organization has trained hundreds of educators in our region to be leaders in their schools.

Although our organization has trained so many potential leaders, I was still worried about finding 30 people in the region who were skilled enough to lead the home groups at the summer education summit. Having home groups would be a hallmark of this event, and the planning committee had agreed on these goals for the home group participants:

- Join in collaborative inquiry and reflection.
- Share ideas and learn from multiple perspectives.
- Develop a deeper understanding of the institute's outcomes.
- Work in a professional learning community setting.

This was a tall order. This summit would be open to anyone who wanted to come, and we wanted everybody to have a powerful learning experience so that they would be encouraged to go back to their own campuses or workplaces and institute more reflection and collaboration.

From past experiences at similar conferences, we knew that there would be a full spectrum of experience levels in our home groups: Many of the participants would be familiar with the concepts and lingo of being in a professional learning community, some might have just heard about it, and a few would be parents or community members who weren't working in schools and would have no idea what we were talking about if we threw around abbreviations like "CFG" or "PLC."

DESCRIBING POWERFUL FACILITATION

In order to get feedback on how to proceed, I invited six local facilitators whom I really admired for a preplanning session. I wanted to pick their brains to discern what the important traits of skillful facilitators were.

Because they all worked in schools, we met after work hours at my house. We enjoyed gourmet pizza from our favorite coal-fired pizzeria while we reconnected. After we cleared the dishes and refilled our drinks, I asked everyone to get comfortable and get out their journals.

I said, "I've invited you here this evening to get some input on planning the summit that will take place in a few months. Before we start planning, I want us to get in the mindset for thinking about great facilitation. So write about a time when you experienced powerful facilitation. Flesh it out. What was the occasion? Why were you there? What did the facilitator say? What did they do? What did they ask you to do? How did you feel? Let's write for about 10 minutes."

It didn't take long for everyone to think of an instance when they experienced powerful facilitation. Soon, they were all concentrating on re-creating their experiences.

When the sound of pens scratching paper tapered off, I continued, "Form triads for sharing your stories. As one person reads, the other two should listen attentively. After the presenter finishes reading, ask one or two clarifying questions if you need to. Then ask yourselves why the experience was meaningful, what made this experience so different from others like it, and what traits of excellent facilitation emerge from these memories."

There was a buzz in the room while the triads shared, listened, questioned, and discussed. After about half an hour, we reconvened in a big circle and shared out.

Bea said, "In the experience that I wrote about, the facilitator asked such thoughtful questions. The questions really pushed my thinking."

Miguel added, "For me, my powerful experience happened when the facilitator listened—really listened."

Myrtle said, "Good facilitators can plan a thoughtful agenda and move seamlessly from activity to activity. But the great ones remember to allow time for reflection."

"It's not just what they do," offered Artie. "It seems to me that the best facilitators have a particular way of being. They have a way of making everyone feel comfortable."

"Well, I agree that a great facilitator is pleasant, positive, and flexible," said Dennis. "But they take the work very seriously. They don't let a desire for comfort get in the way of doing important transformative work."

"To use a metaphor from my chemistry classroom, they're like catalysts," replied Glenda. "They get things started, but they get out of the way. Somehow, they make things happen, but remain neutral."

While I scribed on a piece of chart paper, we went around again and again. Our conversation deepened as we teased out what effective facilitators know and do and talked about how we ourselves could embody those traits as we planned powerful home group experiences for the people who would attend the summer education summit.

WHAT FACILITATORS KNOW

My facilitator friends had brought so many important facilitator traits to life. After they left, I continued to chew on what they had said and then went to my bookshelf to round out the picture of skilled facilitation that was forming in my mind.

So many of the books about facilitation that I owned were from the business world, where a facilitator is defined as the person who focuses on the process of meetings (Ghais, 2005). As Myrtle had said, a facilitator knows how to plan a thoughtful agenda with a variety of activities, and several books on my shelf presented step-by-step guides, checklists, and worksheets to help business facilitators solve problems and make decisions (Bens, 2005; Justice & Jamieson, 2012).

However, it seemed like the facilitators I was seeking for the education summit would also need to be well versed in the context of schooling in our region and have a wide-ranging familiarity with protocols that were specific to school contexts.

WHAT FACILITATORS DO

During our activity, Bea and Miguel had mentioned facilitator skills such as listening and questioning. I found that *The Facilitator's Book of Questions: Tools for Looking Together at Student Work* (Allen & Blythe, 2004) explained that facilitators must attend to the learning, logistics, and longevity of their groups. Attending to learning would include planning meaningful agendas and facilitating protocols. Logistics would include arranging for meeting time, space, and food and making sure that all materials were available. Attending to longevity would include encouraging commitment to the work and continuously improving by seeking feedback about one's facilitation and reflecting about it.

A quote from *Advanced Facilitation Strategies: Tools and Techniques to Master Difficult Situations* (Bens, 2005) summed it up best:

> The main goal of all facilitation activities is to enhance the effectiveness of others, whether that's the personal effectiveness of an individual who is being coached, the ability of a team to reach its goals, or the overall wellness of an organization and its culture. (p. 3)

Whatever facilitators do, it is always in the service of others' learning.

WHO FACILITATORS ARE

What intrigued me most about the traits of powerful facilitation that my friends had developed was that they went beyond knowledge and action. There was a strong sense that the personal presence of the facilitator—being pleasant, positive, flexible, yet serious—had an important influence on the work of the group. This hunch was better explained by Suzanne Ghais (2005) in her book *Extreme Facilitation: Guiding Groups Through Controversy and Complexity*. As I flipped through this book again, I saw that Ghais's framework of "capacities" that a facilitator must strive for was a good place to start to understand who facilitators are.

According to Ghais, *physical capacity* refers to bringing positive energy to your group and making sure that needs for nourishment, light, fresh air, and a pleasant meeting space are met. I'm sure that getting special pizzas and meeting at my home contributed to the rich discussion that we had. *Emotional capacity* refers to welcoming and working with feelings rather than subverting them, and *intellectual capacity* refers to being able to deal with complex issues.

What intrigued me most was the idea that facilitators needed an *intuitive capacity* that could help spark insights and ideas. I thought that this would be especially important at our summer summit, where we would bring together many stakeholders who were passionate about improving education. Each home group would have teachers and principals from schools across the region. We hoped to have representatives from higher education, policymakers, and even high school students in the groups as well. This could be a wonderful opportunity for gaining insights into the issues that we faced.

The final capacity is *spiritual*, which includes exhorting people to be their best and building a sense of community. These were all things that I aspired to be.

FACILITATION IS A DEVELOPMENTAL PROCESS

With all this reading and reflecting, I realized that I couldn't just put out a request for applications to the local community and expect to get 30 facilitators who already had all these skills and capacities. My model for recruiting facilitators would have to include a training component. People might look good on paper, but I wouldn't know what they were capable of until I saw them in action.

How could I build on my current system of training and support to develop a cadre of reflective facilitators who continuously sought out ways to improve what they know and what they do as well as transform who they are?

Chapter 11 Discussion Questions

What?

1. Jacob is just beginning to draft his own framework for understanding facilitative practices. What does Jacob think facilitators should know, should do, and should be like?
2. What would you add to Jacob's framework? What does effective facilitation look like to you?

So What?

3. The thread that connects the dilemmas in this book puts emphasis on the role of the facilitator. Reexamine the cases with Jacob's facilitation framework in mind. What does each facilitator know? What do they do? What personal qualities do they have that help them be effective facilitators?

  a. Chapters 2–4, Andrea
  b. Chapter 5, Elnara
  c. Chapter 6, Darlene
  d. Chapter 7, Juling
  e. Chapter 8, Reginald
  f. Chapter 9, Lannitra
  g. Chapter 10, Debbie
  h. Chapter 11, Jacob

Now What?

4. Now that you have read the cases in this book, reexamine the philosophy of facilitation that you wrote when you studied Chapter 2, "Becoming a Facilitator." Has your philosophy of facilitation changed? What additions, deletions, or changes might you make?
5. Where do you experience tension in your own practice as a facilitative leader?
6. Consider writing up your experiences as a case study. What is the context? Who are the main characters? What are the salient conflicts?

   Does writing about your experience help you see things from a different perspective?

Scaffolding for Discussion Questions

Each case study concludes with discussion questions that are designed to help the reader identify facilitative skills and strategies, make connections to his or her own work as a facilitative leader, and encourage reflection on possible changes in practice.

The following charts are intended to broaden your perspective and spark discussion. They are not exhaustive. A blank template is provided so you can make copies and take notes while you read each chapter.

Chapter ____: _____

Description What do I observe?	Interpretation What are the implications? Why is this important?

Chapter 2: Becoming a Facilitator

Description What do I observe?	Interpretation What are the implications? Why is this important?
The critical friends groups are voluntary.	How might being voluntary or required affect the nature of a learning community?
Group members have little in common.	How does the makeup of a group's personnel affect its purpose and goals?
Facilitator reuses agendas from training sessions.	How do facilitators craft agendas?
Facilitator uses the reflective prompt "What worked? What didn't work? What do you need?"	What is the purpose of written reflections? What kinds of prompts elicit useful reflection?
Facilitator meets with other trained facilitators.	In what ways do facilitators get support and guidance?
Group meets once a month for 2 hours after school.	What is the minimum amount of time that a group can meet in order to accomplish its goals? How do the meeting time and place affect the atmosphere of the meeting?
Facilitator writes a personal philosophy of facilitation.	What is the purpose of a philosophy of facilitation? How can it help a facilitator?
More observations . . .	*More implications . . .*

Chapter 3: Becoming Questioners

Description What do I observe?	Interpretation What are the implications? Why is this important?
Facilitator has a close personal relationship with one of the group members.	How do personal relationships enrich or constrain professional relationships?
Facilitator presents student work from own classroom.	What is the role of modeling in learning new habits?
Tuning protocol includes both warm and cool feedback.	What is the right balance of warm and cool feedback?
Group members question if examining student work helps the teacher.	What are realistic expectations for improving work by examining it?
Group member makes a laughing comment.	How can a facilitator interpret the meaning of comments? When should a facilitator intervene?
Facilitator refers to feedback norms.	How do norms contribute to the professional atmosphere?
Group member volunteers to present best practices related to digital writing assignments.	What kinds of conversations should take place in CFGs? In PLCs? At department meetings? At workshops?
Facilitator examines written reflections.	How can a facilitator gain insight about group members?
Facilitator and group member meet for a preconference.	What is the purpose of the preconference? What topics might come up during a preconference?
Group uses the term *chief inquirer* instead of *presenter*.	How do the terms we use affect our expectations?
More observations . . .	*More implications . . .*

Chapter 4: Becoming Listeners

Description What do I observe?	Interpretation What are the implications? Why is this important?
Facilitator uses protocols to frame professional conversations.	What are the benefits of using protocols? What features make protocols uncomfortable for some members?
Group meets for 2 hours each month.	How do educators make the most of limited time for professional development?
Facilitator chooses to try the Collaborative Assessment Conference.	How do facilitators choose the best protocol for a particular need? How do facilitators learn new protocols?
The group has members from several content areas.	What can teachers in different content areas learn from one another?
Resistant member is an early-career math teacher.	How might stage of career or content area affect what kinds of professional development are needed or desired?
Resistant member conceptualizes protocols as barriers.	How might a facilitator explain protocols in a variety of ways?
Facilitator aspires to have a less abrupt style.	How does facilitation style affect group members' reactions to protocols?
More observations . . .	*More implications . . .*

Chapter 5: Engaging a Reluctant Team Member

Description What do I observe?	Interpretation What are the implications? Why is this important?
Groups are structured with members who don't regularly work together.	How does the composition of a group affect community building and commitment?
Facilitators get input and agreement from group members about meeting times.	How can facilitators build shared commitment within a group?
Facilitators are aware of unequal participation patterns. Awareness of verbal communication patterns such as flat tone Awareness of nonverbal communication patterns (does not talk, bored expression, limited eye contact, pairing with carpool partner)	How can closely attending to communication patterns give insight into what group members are thinking? Do facilitators make accurate assumptions about the meaning of verbal and nonverbal communication patterns?
Facilitators encourage participant to go home when he felt ill.	When is it appropriate to be flexible?
Facilitators delay several months before confronting participant about disengaged behaviors.	What are the barriers to assertive facilitation?
Facilitators bring their problem to a group of colleagues for feedback.	How can communities of practice enrich an individual's work?
Facilitators meet with disengaged group member at his own workplace.	How can shaking up expectations and habits lead to new learning?
More observations . . .	*More implications . . .*

Chapter 6: Dealing with Difficult People

Description What do I observe?	Interpretation What are the implications? Why is this important?
Parent organization has a three-part mission statement.	How might having a mission statement affect a group's focus?
Every person on the board has a well-defined role.	How does a group's structure affect its effectiveness?
President facilitates 3-2-1 icebreaker at first board meeting.	What is the purpose of icebreakers and team builders? What can be learned from them?
Treasurer prioritizes work and family over Band Booster obligations.	How can leaders balance work, family, and volunteer opportunities?
Vice president is "ticked off" by delays to project.	How do groups prioritize initiatives? How is the priority communicated?
President constructs meeting agenda to address understanding different work styles.	What is the purpose of meeting? How can leaders address concerns about how group members work together?
VP walks out of Compass Points activity.	How does a facilitator choose what behaviors to respond to?
VP suggests that president "plays around too much" in meetings.	What are the different purposes that a meeting might have? What kinds of activities are appropriate for business meetings?
President listens to VP and projects neutral stance.	What are some strategies for defusing tense situations?
More observations . . .	*More implications . . .*

Chapter 7: Navigating Conflict

Description What do I observe?	Interpretation What are the implications? Why is this important?
Facilitator meets with client to negotiate contract and customize seminar.	What should be discussed during the contracting phase?
Supervisor appoints somebody to negotiate details of the agenda.	How can a facilitator make sure that the decisionmakers have all the information they need?
Norms address long-term collaboration.	Are there any nonnegotiables for what should be included in group norms?
Chalk Talk highlights tension about shared vision.	How should facilitators respond when new issues emerge?
Supervisor is not present for part of training.	What are the expectations for attendance? Are different members held to different standards for attendance?
Facilitator is distracted by personal problems.	What are a facilitator's responsibilities for attending to the feelings of group members?
Facilitator realizes that activity is causing distress.	How can a facilitator both push a group to examine assumptions and attend to feelings?
Facilitator writes in a personal journal.	What tools can a facilitator use for self-reflection?
Facilitator and supervisor meet one-on-one.	What kinds of communications are best done face-to-face? Over email? By phone?
Group reads article about stages of team development.	What texts should a facilitator be familiar with?
More observations . . .	*More implications . . .*

Chapter 8: Reclaiming Professional Identity

Description What do I observe?	Interpretation What are the implications? Why is this important?
Department chair looks forward to coffee and cake at a meeting.	What is the role of hospitality in creating a collegial work environment?
Individual teacher bonuses are published.	What policies might motivate teachers to improve?
Bonuses are calculated with a formula that is not public.	What is the role of transparency in cultivating trust?
Department members mention field trips, contests, student engagement, and special events related to the curriculum.	What is valid evidence that a content department is thriving?
Department applies for teacher research grant.	What is the role of external funding in influencing the work in schools?
Department members agree on research question.	How can collaborative teacher inquiry focus the work of teachers?
Grant winners from across the region meet together.	How does reducing isolation increase professionalism?
More observations . . .	*More implications . . .*

Chapter 9: Honoring Time to Meet and Incorporating Technology

Description What do I observe?	Interpretation What are the implications? Why is this important?
Group members receive a stipend for attendance.	How might financial incentives affect professional development?
Facilitator prefers face-to-face meetings.	What are the advantages and disadvantages of virtual meetings?
Facilitator maps concept of reflective practice onto research concepts.	How can a facilitator mitigate resistance to reflective practices?
Facilitator asks group members if they can meet on a different day, at a different time, or in a different way.	What values determine who gets accommodated?
Group member has conflict caused by principal's demands.	Who has the ultimate power to decide which meetings are most important?
Meeting attendance plummets.	Is there a minimum number of people needed to have a fruitful meeting?
One member attends regular meeting through a video call.	How does having virtual meetings affect the role of the facilitator? What about planning?
Facilitator posts reflections on blog.	How can group members reinforce learning in between meetings?
Blog is public.	What are appropriate boundaries for making reflective work public and keeping it safe?
More observations . . .	*More implications . . .*

Chapter 10: Developing Cultural Competence

Description What do I observe?	Interpretation What are the implications? Why is this important?
School system offers "culture training" to teacher leaders.	How can a school system support cross-cultural understanding?
Norms are posted in room.	What is the role of norms in creating a safe space for cross-cultural conversation?
Most of the participants in the narrator's group are strangers.	What kinds of settings are conducive to difficult conversations?
White man is not allowed to speak in small group.	How can facilitators surface assumptions about identity and privilege?
Teacher reflects about her personal background.	How does self-knowledge enrich cross-cultural understanding? How might focusing on individual circumstances reduce sensitivity to systemic inequality?
Small group engages in activity based on "White Privilege: Unpacking the Invisible Knapsack."	What resources and activities can be used to promote cross-cultural dialogue?
Teaching colleagues engage in "Cultural Conversations."	What are the qualities of transformative professional development?
More observations . . .	*More implications . . .*

Chapter 11: Conclusion: Reflecting on the Role of the Facilitator

Description What do I observe?	Interpretation What are the implications? Why is this important?
Facilitator invites colleagues to join him for a preplanning session.	What is the role of planning in conducting successful meetings or events?
Facilitator develops a process of writing, sharing, listening, and reflecting to discern the qualities of powerful facilitation.	How do facilitators create new protocols?
Facilitator consults relevant books and articles.	How important is it to maintain a professional library?
Facilitators discern that personal qualities influence a facilitator's work.	How might facilitators transform themselves?
Facilitator decides to add a training component to the recruiting plan.	What kinds of ongoing training and support do facilitators need at different times in their careers?
More observations . . .	*More implications . . .*

Resources

Chapter 2: Becoming a Facilitator

This chapter draws heavily from concepts articulated in "The Zen of Facilitation" (Killion & Simmons, 1992).

The inspiration to write out a personal philosophy of facilitation comes from *Advanced Facilitation Strategies: Tools and Techniques to Master Difficult Situations* (Bens, 2005).

The School Reform Initiative supports the development of transformational adult learning communities. Hundreds of protocols and links to other helpful resources can be found on their website at http://www.schoolreform-initiative.org.

Chapter 3: Becoming Questioners

The characters in this chapter demonstrate that they have widely different motivations for joining the critical friends group. The book *Leading for Powerful Learning: A Guide for Instructional Leaders* (Breidenstein, Fahey, Glickman, & Hensley, 2012) provides suggestions for professional development.

Chapter 4: Becoming Listeners

Several books address using protocols to enhance professional conversations. My favorites include *Looking Together at Student Work* (Blythe, Allen, & Powell, 2008) and *The Power of Protocols: An Educator's Guide to Better Practice* (McDonald, Mohr, Dichter, & McDonald, 2007).

The School Reform Initiative curates a wide-ranging collection of protocols at www.schoolreforminitiative.org.

Chapter 5: Engaging a Reluctant Team Member

Both Ingrid Bens's (2005) *Advanced Facilitation Strategies: Tools and Techniques to Master Difficult Situations* and Daniel Venables's (2011) *The Practice of Authentic PLCs: A Guide to Effective Teacher Teams* include scenarios to help facilitators anticipate challenges such as disengaged participants.

Chapter 6: Dealing with Difficult People

Interactions: Collaboration Skills for School Professionals (Friend & Cook, 2003), especially Chapter 11, "Difficult Interactions," offers many helpful strategies for understanding and dealing with resistance.

Chapter 7: Navigating Conflict

Suzanne Ghais's (2005) book *Extreme Facilitation: Guiding Groups Through Controversy and Complexity* describes the personal capacities (physical, emotional, intellectual, intuitive, and spiritual) that facilitators must cultivate in themselves and in the groups with which they work. Ghais also gives an account of the steps in the contracting process so that many misunderstandings can be avoided.

The article "Stages of Team Development" (Mohr & Dichter, 2002) that the group members read in this case is available at http://www.annenberginstitute.org/pdf/Stages.pdf.

Chapter 8: Reclaiming Professional Identity

Many of the instructional changes that appear in this chapter come from *120 Content Strategies for English Language Learners: Teaching for Academic Success in Secondary School* (Reiss, 2012) and *Classroom Instruction That Works with English Language Learners* (Hill & Flynn, 2006).

Chapter 9: Honoring Time to Meet and Incorporating Technology

The idea of helping science teachers embrace reflective practice by mapping it onto accepted science concepts was inspired by the article "A Design-Based Self-Study of the Development of Student Reflection in Teacher Education" in *Studying Teacher Education* by Aubusson, Griffin, and Steele (2010).

The book *Going Online with Protocols: New Tools for Teaching and Learning* (McDonald, Mannheimer Zydney, Dichter, & McDonald, 2012) includes encouragement and specific strategies for facilitating an online learning community.

Chapter 10: Developing Cultural Competence

Several books influenced the development of this chapter. Especially notable were *We Can't Teach What We Don't Know: White Teachers, Multiracial Schools* (Howard, 1999); *Everyday Antiracism: Getting Real About Race in School* (Pollock, 2008); *Courageous Conversations About Race: A Field Guide for Achieving Equity in Schools* (Singleton & Linton, 2006); and *Can We Talk About Race?: And Other Conversations in an Era of School Resegregation* (Tatum, 2007).

Chapter 11: Conclusion: Reflecting on the Role of the Facilitator

The gold standard for understanding the facilitation of groups using protocols continues to be *The Facilitator's Book of Questions: Tools for Looking Together at Student and Teacher Work* (Allen & Blythe, 2004).

References

Achinstein, B. (2002). Conflict amid community: The micropolitics of teacher collaboration. *Teachers College Record, 104*(3), 421–455.

Allen, D., & Blythe, T. (2004). *The facilitator's book of questions: Tools for looking together at student and teacher work.* New York, NY: Teachers College Press.

Aubusson, P., Griffin, J., & Steele, F. (2010). A design-based self-study of the development of student reflection in teacher education. *Studying Teacher Education, 6*(2), 201–216.

Banks, J. A. (2007). *Educating citizens in a multicultural society* (2nd ed.). New York, NY: Teachers College Press.

Bateson, M. C. (1994). *Peripheral visions.* New York, NY: HarperCollins.

Bens, I. (2005). *Advanced facilitation strategies: Tools and techniques to master difficult situations.* San Francisco, CA: Jossey-Bass.

Blythe, T., Allen, D., & Powell, B. S. (2008). *Looking together at student work* (2nd ed.). New York, NY: Teachers College Press.

Bolam, R., McMahon, A., Stoll, L., Thomas, S., & Wallace, M. (2005). *Creating and sustaining effective professional learning communities* (Research Report No. 637). Bristol, UK: University of Bristol.

Breidenstein, A., Fahey, K., Glickman, C., & Hensley, F. (2012). *Leading for powerful learning: A guide for instructional leaders.* New York, NY: Teachers College Press.

Clandinin, D. J., & Connelly, F. M. (Eds.). (1995). *Teachers' professional knowledge landscapes.* New York, NY: Teachers College Press.

Clandinin, D. J., Huber, J., Huber, M., Murphy, M. S., Murray Orr, A., Pearce, M., & Steeves, P. (2006). *Composing diverse identities: Narrative inquiries into the interwoven lives of children and teachers.* New York, NY: Routledge.

Conzemius, A., & O'Neill, J. (2001). *Building shared responsibility for student learning.* Alexandria, VA: Association for Supervision and Curriculum Development.

Craig, C. J. (2003). *Narrative inquiries of school reform: Storied lives, storied landscapes, storied metaphors.* Greenwich, CT: Information Age Publishing.

Craig, C. J. (2007). Illuminating qualities of knowledge communities in a portfolio-making context. *Teachers and Teaching: Theory and Practice, (13)*6, 617–636.

Curry, M. (2008). Critical Friends Groups: The possibilities and limitations embedded in teacher professional communities aimed at instructional improvement and school reform. *Teachers College Record, 110*(4), 733–774.

Dewey, J. (1938). *Education and experience.* New York, NY: Collier Books.

Díaz-Maggioli, G. (2004). *Teacher-centered professional development.* Alexandria, VA: Association for Supervision and Curriculum Development.

DuFour, R. (2005). What is a professional learning community? In R. DuFour, R. Eaker, & R. DuFour (Eds.), *On common ground: The power of professional learning communities* (pp. 31–43). Bloomington, IN: Solution Tree.

DuFour, R., DuFour, R., & Eaker, R. (2008). *Revisiting professional learning communities at work: New insights for improving schools.* Bloomington, IN: Solution Tree.

DuFour, R., DuFour, R., Eaker, R., & Karhanek, G. (2004). *Whatever it takes: How professional learning communities respond when kids don't learn.* Bloomington, IN: Solution Tree.

DuFour, R., & Eaker, R. (1998). *Professional learning communities at work: Best practices for enhancing student achievement.* Bloomington, IN: National Education Service.

Easton, L. B. (2008). From professional development to professional learning. *Phi Delta Kappan, 89*(10), 755–761.

Ellinger, M. (2008). Increasing elementary teachers' fundamental math content knowledge and developing a collaborative faculty. In A. Lieberman & L. Miller (Eds.), *Teachers in professional communities: Improving teaching and learning* (pp. 73–84). New York, NY: Teachers College Press.

Fahey, K., & Ippolito, J. (2014). Towards a general theory of critical friends groups. Retreived from http://www.schoolreforminitiative.org/wp-content/uploads/2014/02/SRI_General_Theory_CFGs_March_2014_JCI_KF_Website.pdf.

Friend, M., & Cook, L. (2003). *Interactions: Collaboration skills for school professionals* (4th ed.). Boston, MA: Allyn and Bacon.

Ghais, S. (2005). *Extreme facilitation: Guiding groups through controversy and complexity.* San Francisco, CA: Jossey-Bass.

Goddard, Y., Goddard, R., & Tschannen-Moran, M. (2007). A theoretical and empirical investigation of teacher collaboration for school improvement and student achievement in public elementary schools. *Teachers College Record, 109*(4), 877–896.

Grossman, P., Wineburg, S., & Woolworth, S. (2001). Toward a theory of teacher community. *Teachers College Record, 103*(6), 943–1012.

Hill, J. D., & Flynn, K. M. (2006). *Classroom instruction that works with English Language Learners.* Alexandria, VA: Asociation for Supervision and Curriculum Development.

Hord, S. M. (Ed.). (2004). *Learning together, leading together: Changing schools through professional learning communities.* New York, NY: Teachers College Press.

Howard, G. R. (1999). *We can't teach what we don't know: White teachers, multiracial schools.* New York, NY: Teachers College Press.

Ingersoll, R., & Smith, T. (2003). The wrong solution to the teacher shortage. *Educational Leadership, 60*(8), 30–33.

Justice, T., & Jamieson, D. W. (2012). *The facilitator's fieldbook* (3rd ed.). New York, NY: American Management Association.

Killion, J. P., & Simmons, L. A. (1992). The Zen of facilitation. *Journal of Staff Development, 13*(3), 2–5.

Lieberman, A., & Miller, L. (Eds.). (2008). *Teachers in professional communities: Improving teaching and learning.* New York, NY: Teachers College Press.

McDonald, J. P., Mannheimer Zydney, J., Dichter, A., & McDonald, E. C. (2012). *Going online with protocols: New tools for teaching and learning.* New York, NY: Teachers College Press.

McDonald, J. P., Mohr, N., Dichter, A., & McDonald, E. C. (2007). *The power of protocols: An educator's guide to better practice* (2nd ed.). New York, NY: Teachers College Press.

McIntosh, P. (1989, July/August). White privilege: Unpacking the invisible knapsack. *Peace and Freedom,* 10–12.

McLaughlin, M. W., & Talbert, J. E. (2001). *Professional communities and the work of high school teaching.* Chicago, IL: University of Chicago Press.

Merseth, K. K. (1996). Cases and case methods in teacher education. In J. Sikula (Ed.), *Handbook of research on teacher education* (2nd ed.) (pp. 722–746). New York, NY: Macmillan/Simon & Schuster.

Mohr, N., & Dichter, A. (2002). *Stages of team development: Lessons from the struggles of site-based management.* Providence, RI: Annenberg Institute for School Reform.

Payne, C. M. (2008). *So much reform, so little change: The persistence of failure in urban schools.* Cambridge, MA: Harvard Education Press.

Pollock, M. (Ed.). (2008). *Everyday antiracism: Getting real about race in school.* New York, NY: New Press.

Putnam, R. D. (2007). *E pluribus unum*: Diversity and community in the twenty-first century. *Scandinavian Political Studies, 30*(2), 137–174.

Ramsey, P. G. (2004). *Teaching and learning in a diverse world* (3rd ed.). New York, NY: Teachers College Press.

Reiss, J. (2012). *120 content strategies for English Language Learners: Teaching for academic success in secondary school* (2nd ed.). New York, NY: Pearson.

Schön, D. A. (1987). *Educating the reflective practitioner: Toward a new design for teaching and learning in the professions.* San Francisco, CA: Jossey-Bass.

School Reform Initiative (SRI). (2014). *SRI resource and protocol book.* Denver, CO: School Reform Initiative.

Singleton, G. E., & Linton, C. (2006). *Courageous conversations about race: A field guide for achieving equity in schools.* Thousand Oaks, CA: Corwin.

Tatum, B. D. (2007). *Can we talk about race?: And other conversations in an era of school resegregation.* Boston, MA: Beacon Press.

Thompson-Grove, G. (2005, January). *A call to action*. Keynote address given at the 9th Annual NSRF Winter Meeting, Cambridge, MA.

Venables, D. R. (2011). *The practice of authentic PLCs: A guide to effective teacher teams.* Thousand Oaks, CA: Corwin.

Wenger, E., McDermott, R., & Snyder, W. M. (2002). *Cultivating communities of practice.* Boston, MA: Harvard Business School Press.

Wood, D. (2007). Teachers' learning communities: Catalyst for change or a new infrastructure for the status quo? *Teachers College Record, 109*(3), 699–739.

Index

About the Author

Donna J. Reid is an educational consultant, critical friends group coach for the Houston Independent School District, and lecturer in the College of Education at the University of Houston. Previously, she taught history and English at Johnston Middle School in Houston, Texas, and also served her campus as a department chair, team leader, school portfolio chairperson, and critical friends group coach. Her research interests include reflective practice, facilitation, and teacher research. She regularly presents at national and international conferences and facilitates workshops and seminars where educators can deepen and strengthen their reflection and collaboration skills.